To Bay...
Valentines...
with much
Love
Kim

LOVE & WAR

LOVE & WAR

250 Years of Wartime Love Letters

BY

SUSAN BESZE WALLACE

THE SUMMIT PUBLISHING GROUP

THE SUMMIT PUBLISHING GROUP
One Arlington Centre, 1112 East Copeland Road, Fifth Floor
Arlington, Texas 76011

Printed in the United States of America.

01 00 99 98 97   010 5 4 3 2 1

Library of Congress Cataloging-in-Publication Data
Love & war : 250 years of wartime love letters / [compiled] by Susan Besze Wallace.
   p. cm.
  ISBN 1-56530-219-2
   1. United States—History, Military—Sources. 2. Soldiers—United
States—Correspondence. 3. Love-letters—United States.
I. Wallace, Susan Besze, 1969-   . II. Title: Love and war.
E181.L84 1996
355.1'0973—dc21   97-4848
                                      CIP

Photo Credits

In addition to the photographs sent by family and friends (see acknowldgements) the publisher gratefully acknowledges the following for permission to publish the photographs on the pages specified.

Josh Parsons (pages 74-75)
National Archives (pages vi, 2-3, 10-16, 19, 20, 21, 23, 26-27, 29 (two photos), 42-43, 49, 56-57, 60 (two photos), 69, 70).
National Portrait Gallery, Smithsonian Institution (pages 6-7).
PhotoAssist (pages 9, 19 (map), 32-33, 38, 52,)
Rhode Island Historical Society (pages vi, 17).

WWI postcards courtesy of The Museum of Valor, Spotsylvania, Virginia.

Antiques courtesy of The Sampler Antique & Design Mall, 1715 E. Lamar Blvd. Arlington, Tx 76006
Photography of antiques by Robin Sherman-Dean

Cover and book design by Dennis Davidson

Dedicated to all the men and women
who have served our country,
and the love that sustained them.

God be with you

DEPARTMENT OF DE...
UNITED STATE...

For Correspondence

Just thought i would ... a card that i am prettie ... Nel and hope to be with you Soon for i am going to get a furloaf and So i hope it all ...

For Add...

Mrs. Elizabeth Lankh...
#629 Burns Str...
Cincinnati
Ohio

Soldier Lovers 12 des.

403

...actions, ... people who are not ... often do not realize what ... motives may be ascribed ... them. If I have ... made my meaning ... clear, I am perfectly ... willing to leave to ... your judgment ... entire future ... I have in your ... ment complete ...

J.C.MERTIC

Contents

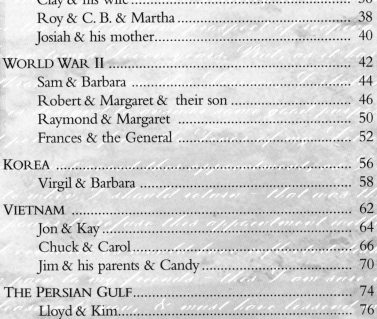

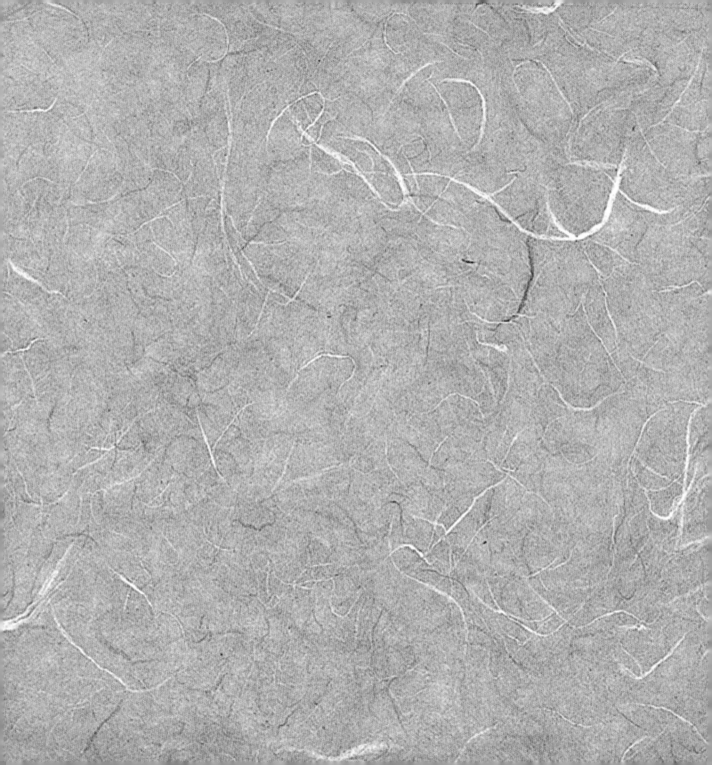

ACKNOWLEDGMENTS

Dozens of people trusted me with their past, sharing intimate details of wartime relationships and sometimes reliving painful memories unearthed by their love letters. More than thanks, they are owed great tribute. Preserving their personal history here only begins to honor their service and their sacrifice.

Much gratitude to James and Candace Young, whose friendship will touch me every Christmas; Lloyd and Kimberley Aucoin; Mary Bedard; Virgil Price; Roy and Kathy Bolar; John and Joy Chavez, may your trials be outweighed by your triumphs; Alex W. Jerome; Robert Loring and his romantic parents; Kristopher Ligget and Lucinda R. Ligget, proud descendants of George Granville Sharp; fellow Horned Frog, Kay Merkel Boruff; Virginia Messick, Fredericksburg, Virginia; Mary S. Drader, La Crescentia, California; Sam and Barbara Head, Macon, Georgia; Carol Shahan, Fremont, California, and the venerable Rowe family of Fredericksburg, Virginia, which has given me much more than the use of letters.

It should be noted that some of the photos in this book depict people and objects representative of the periods when these letter were written. Not every image near a letter is of the people who wrote the letters or of objects belonging to them.

Many people supported this endeavor in spirit, if not with personal correspondence. I was propelled by their enthusiasm and grateful for their assistance and that of their institutions: The Museum of Valor, Wayne and Jerry Hart, Spotsylvania, Virginia; The Marine Corps Historical Center, Amy Cantin, Washington, D.C.; Naval Historical Collection, Dr. Evelyn Cherpak, Naval War College, Newport, Rhode Island; Virginia Historical Society, Richmond, Va.; Rhode Island Historical Society, Manuscript Collection, Providence, Rhode Island; Mount Vernon Ladies Association, Mount Vernon, Virginia; Anne Webb, The Tudor Place Foundation, Washington, D.C.; and *Recollections and Letters of Robert E. Lee*, Doubleday Doran & Co., 1903, 1924.

Special thanks to my husband, Todd, a U.S. marine whose presence in my life is like getting a love letter every day.

POST CARD

Series 596 Soldier Lovers 12 des.

CHARLOTTE, N.C.
6 AM
1918

For Correspondence

To My Dear Girl. Apr the

Just thought i Would you
a card that i am prettie
Nel and hope to be With
you Soon fore i am
going to git a furloaf and
i am coming to Sea you
So i hope it Wil be very sun
fore i Would like to Sea your
Sweat littel face cloon fore
i dont think that thay ever Wil
nead us anie more down Trance
fore the Germans are all killed
So dont Warie Dear fore i know
Som von is cauling me and
i gas it is you by by from L.K.
ad

For Address

Miss Elizabeth Lankheet,
#629 Burns Street,
Cincinnatie
Ohio.

A Passionate Tradition

There are love affairs going on under beds, in shoe boxes, and atop closet shelves across this country. Some are recklessly passionate, brimming with promises and pronouncements of everlasting love. Others are more reserved, offering deceptively passive hellos and good-byes punctuated by a few Xs and Os—and the stamp of a military censor.

Love letters predate the post office and outlive their senders and recipients; but love letters written during wartime do much, much more.

From the letters ·George Washington hand-inked to Martha to the postcards sent to sweethearts from the Persian Gulf, these missives are living history. They tell the human story behind the wars we studied in school. They trace the changing nature of men and women's roles in society. They manifest the power of love and hope, amid tragedy.

Decade after decade, American men and women have been called upon to serve their country. Letters have been their reinforcements. They preserve a soldier's sanity. They strengthen a young wife's courage. They serve as a lifeline between lovers.

Letters distract servicemen from death and destruction, if only briefly. They give soldiers a place to pour their angst, lest they drown in it. Receiving letters reassures them that home exists, and that someone there is eager to embrace their exhausted, filthy selves. Some veterans say that writing a lover—about the bitter cold, the death of a friend, the confusion of killing—made the surreal nature of war very real indeed, and helped them confront their own mortality. Many women were surprised at the depth of emotion revealed by such letters from camp, trench, or aircraft carrier. Men who were normally very reserved dug deep inside, using a parade of new pet names and writing things they might not have been able to say face-to-face.

But not every woman was so fortunate, and many nagged at their husbands to write more. They often needed more than sweet talk. During World War II, women were left alone to deal with things like car maintenance, life insurance policies, and filing taxes, not to mention raising children. Today, women write letters from the front lines, not just the home front.

Reading the most passionate love letters turns us into human thermometers, the "mercury" rising up from our toes, washing over our hearts until finally our brain tingles with the realization that these words were arranged this way just for us. Unlike a telephone call, letters take commitment and concentration. They're like paper kisses, some short and sweet, others long and deep.

Steamy young lovers aren't the only ones responsible for magic wartime love letters. Married couples longed for each other. Sons waxed nostalgic to their mothers. Servicemen penned letters to newborn children they wouldn't see until toddlerhood. One girl wrote her dead brother's commanding officer in tribute.

There was V-mail during World War II. Now there's E-mail. One might suppose that technology would take some of the steam out of love letters. But during the Persian Gulf war in 1991, the "Any Serviceman" letter-writing campaign saw thousands of envelopes change hands. People wanted to reach out. Strangers got to know each other through words on paper instead of by physical contact. Many met and married as a result.

I've been deeply moved as I relived these moments with those who have dusted off shoe boxes and unfolded musty pages. Join me in sharing their memories—both the sweet and the bitter—in the hope that no one will ever have to write another wartime love letter. Recalling their sacrifices, let's celebrate the power of love—and of patriotism.

THE REVOLUTIONARY WAR

Me, O my, I love him so,
Broke my heart to see him go,
Only time can heal my woe,
Johnny has gone for a soldier.

AMERICAN FOLK SONG OF THE
REVOLUTIONARY WAR PERIOD

David & Mehitabel

From David Hall
to Mehitabel Tichnor Hall

BERGEN AUGUST 12 1776

Dear and Loving Wife,

I have but a few moments time to write you I would inform you that through the good-nefs of God I am in good health at presant as I hope these Lines will find you...you inform me that you wanted Some tee I went to a great many shops in York when I came Down and I could not hear of any But I have heard Since that there is tee in York I will Send Some as Soon as can... we have not had the victory as yet But we have Lost Long island...I have heard of the heavy Stroke of that Neighbor Swan and his wife has met with in Looseing his Children wich was very Striking to me...I Send my Love to John and hannah and I hope to hear that they have Been good children...

BERGEN OCTOBER 3 1776

…I this moment heard the very meloncholy and surprizing news of your Being very Sick and Both our Children I understand poor John is the worst I hartily pity you under your Dificult and troubelson Sircumstances…I hope to hear Beter news from you next time But I Shall Be afraid to hear I shall Be very uneasy till I hear from you again…I hope I shall not neglect my Duty to put up my hearty petitions to Almighty God for you that it might please him to restore you to health again Your Loving husband David Hall

ENGLISH NEIGHBOURHOOD OCTOBER 7 1776

…I hear it remains very Sickly and Sorrowful times in Litchfield we very often hear Bad news from there gods Judgments in the Land Seems to Call aloud for a universal repentence and mendment..I send my Love to you and my poor Children if they are Living…

ENGLISH NEIGHBOURHOOD OCTOBER 15 1776

…Did I hear John Landon has Lost three of his Children I hope it will please the Lord to preserve our Lives and health that we may See one another again, the time Begins to grow short that we have to stay here…You must not expect Leters from me So often as you have had for paper and ink is very scarce…

ENGLISH NEIGHBOURHOOD OCTOBER 22 1776

…I am very glad to hear that you are all So Comfortable…So you wrote to me that you would have my Shirt Done next week you can send it by Gershorn Gibs of Blue Swamp if you can hear when he comes…I shall ad no more but remain Your

Loving husband
David Hall

DAVID HALL likely never got his shirt. Around November 1, 1776, he and thirty-five other men were placed under the command of Captain Bezaleel Beebe and sent to Fort Washington to aid in its defense. The fort was captured by the enemy and Beebe's company, with the rest of the garrison, were crowded with hundreds of others on board prison ships in Boston Harbor. Hall died December 11, either from hunger and exposure or from smallpox. He is believed to be among the United States' first prisoners of war.

Mehitabel Tichnor Hall returned to Sullivan County, New York, after her husband's death. Son John and daughter Hannah survived their childhood illnesses. Their mother didn't fare as well.

Alexander & Elizabeth

From Alexander Hamilton to Elizabeth Hamilton

AUGUST 1781

In my last letter I informed you that there was a greater prospect of activity now, than there had been heretofore. I did this to prepare your mind for an event, which, I am sure, will give you pain. I begged your father at the same time to intimate to you by degrees the probability of its taking place. I used this method to prevent a surprise which might be too severe to you. A part of the army, my dear girl, is going to Virginia, and I must of necessity be separated at a much greater distance from my beloved wife. I cannot announce the fatal necessity without feeling everything that a fond husband can feel. I am unhappy;- I am unhappy beyond expression. I am unhappy because I am to be so remote from you; because I am to hear from you less frequently than I am accustomed to do. I am

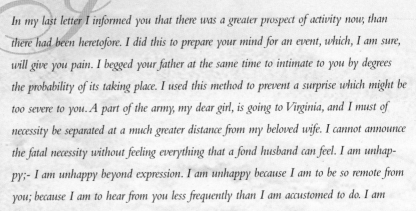

HISTORICAL NOTE

Alexander Hamilton was commissioned a captain in the provincial artillery in 1776. At the Battle of Trenton, he organized his own company and prevented the British under Lord Cornwallis from crossing the Raritan River and attacking George Washington's main army. He was rewarded by being appointed an aide-de-camp at the rank of lieutenant colonel and soon grew into a trusted confidant of General Washington.

Eventually Alexander Hamilton wanted more glory than headquarters could provide, and he pressed George Washington for an active command. He got one, leading an assault on a British stronghold at the siege of Lord Cornwallis's army at Yorktown.

In November 1781, with the war nearly over, Hamilton moved to Albany to study law.

Mrs. Alexander Hamilton

Alexander & Elizabeth

ALEXANDER HAMILTON and Elizabeth Schuyler were married in 1780, and were newlyweds when he sent this letter. They were from very different backgrounds. She hailed from one of New York's most prominent families, while he was forced to begin working at the age of eleven as a merchant's clerk after his father abandoned the family and left his mother destitute. The young man's intense ambition would pay off.

Alexander Hamilton was a New York delegate to the Constitutional Convention in 1787 and also the major author of the *Federalist* papers, essays that had a major influence on the political history of the country. After military service that brought him into George Washington's inner circle, the nation's first president appointed him the first secretary of the United States Treasury.

He died in a duel with political adversary Aaron Burr, who challenged him after some words at a dinner party. Despite his accomplishments, Hamilton, like his own father, left Elizabeth and seven children heavily in debt.

miserable because I know you will be so; I am wretched at the idea of flying so far from you, without a single hour's interview, to tell you all my pains and all my love. But I cannot ask permission to visit you. It might be thought improper to leave my corps at such a time and upon such an occasion. I must go without seeing you, - I must go without embracing you: - alas! I must go. But let no idea, other than of the distance we shall be asunder, disquiet you. Though I said the prospects of activity will be greater, I said it to give your expectations a different turn, and prepare you for something disagreeable. It is ten to one that our views will be disappointed, by Cornwallis retiring to South Carolina by land. At all events, our operations will be over by the latter end of October, and I will fly to my home. Don't mention I am going to Virginia.

George&Martha

From George Washington to Martha Custis Washington

PHILADELPHIA, JUNE 18TH 1775

My Dearest,

I am now set down to write to you on a subject which fills me with inexpressable concern - and this concern is greatly aggravated and Increased when I reflect on the uneasiness I know it will give you - It has been determined in Congress, that the whole Army raised for the defence of the American Cause shall be put under my care, and that it is necessary for me to proceed immediately to Boston to take upon me the Command of it. You may beleive me my dear Patcy, when I asure you, in the most solemn manner, that, so far from seeking this appointment I have used every endeavour in my power to avoid it, not only from my unwillingness to part with you and the Family, but from a consciousness of its being a trust too great for my Capacity, and that I should enjoy more real happiness and felicity in one month with you, at home, than I have the most distant prospect of reaping abroad, if my stay was to be Seven times Seven years. But, as it has been a kind of destiny that has thrown me upon this Service, I shall hope that my under-taking of it, is designd to answer some good purpose - You might, & I suppose did per-ceive, from the Tenor of my Letters, that I was apprehensive I could not avoid this appointment, as I did not even pretend [to] intimate when I should return - that was the case - it was utterly out of my power to refuse this appointment without exposing my Character to such censures as would have reflected dishonour upon myself, and given pain to my friends - this I am sure could not, & ought not to be pleasing to you, & must have lessend me considerably in my own esteem. I shall rely therefore, confidently, on that Prov-idence which has heretofore preservd, & been bountiful to me, not doubting but that I shall return safe to you in the fall - I shall feel no pain from the Toil, or the danger of the Campaign - My unhappiness will flow, from the uneasiness I know you will feel at being left alone - I therefore beg of you to summon your whole fortitude & Resolution,

HISTORICAL NOTE

Shortly after writing his beloved, General Washington assumed command of the Continental Army to lead the colonies to independence. The odds were against him. He forged an army from untrained, often unpaid men and had to cope with a very high turnover rate, due to the short enlistment terms. A harsh winter at Valley Forge proved the ultimate test.

Washington persisted and, with the help of the French army and fleet, pre-vailed. British commander Lord Cornwallis surrendered at Yorktown, Virginia, in 1781.

Washington went on to chair the convention that wrote the United States Constitution. He became the country's first president and earned a place in history as the father of our country.

and pass your time as agreeably as possible - nothing will give me so much sincere satisfaction as to hear this, and to hear it from your own Pen.

If it should be your desire to remove into Alexandria (as you once mentioned upon an occasion of this sort) I am quite pleased that you should put it in practice, & Lund Washington may be redirected, by you, to build a Kitchen and other Houses there proper for your reception - if on the other hand you should rather Incline to spend good part of your time among you Friends below, I wish you to do so - In short, my earnest, & ardent desire is, that you would pursue any Plan that is most likely to produce content, and a tolerable degree of Tranquility as it must add greatly to my uneasy feelings to hear that you are dissatisfied, and complaining at what I really could not avoid.

As Life is always uncertain, and common prudence dictates to every Man the necessity of settling his temporal Concerns whils[t] it is in his power - and whilst the Mind is calm and undistrubed, I have, since I came to this place (for I had not time to do it before I left home) got Colo. Pendleton to Draft a Will for me by the directions which I gave him, which Will I now Inclose - The Provision made for you, in cas[e] of my death, will, I hope, be agreeable; I have Included the Money for which I sold my own Land (to Doctr Mercer) in the Sum given you, as also all other Debts. What I owe myself is very trifling - Cary's Debt excepted, and that would not have been much if the Bank stock had been applied without such difficulties as he made in the Transference.

I shall add nothing more at present as I have several Letters to write, but to desire you will remember me to Milly & all Friends, and to assure you that I am with most unfeigned regard, My dear Patcy Yr Affecte Go: Washington

P.S. Since writing the above I have received your Letter of the 15th and have got two suits of what I was told wa[s] the prettiest Muslin. I wish it may please you—it cost 50/. a suit that is 20/. a yard.

GENERAL WASHINGTON.

George & Martha

These are the only two letters from George Washington to his wife that have survived. It was customary to burn private letters in that day, as they were considered deeply personal. These letters were found in a desk willed to Martha Custis Peter, Martha Washington's granddaughter, after the first first lady's death in 1802.

Martha Dandridge married Daniel Parke Custis in her teens; but her husband died in 1757, leaving her with two small children. Two years later she married George Washington, who raised the boys as his own. Upon returning from the war to Mount Vernon, Washington was faced with tragedy. Jack Custis, his stepson, had died of camp fever in 1781.

PHILADELPHIA, JUNE 23D, 1775

My Dearest,

As I am within a few minutes of leaving this city, I could not think of departing from it without dropping you a line; especially as I do not know whether it may be in my power to write again til I get to the camp at Boston. I go fully trusting in that Providence, which has been more bountiful to me than I deserve, and in full confidence of a happy meeting with you some time in the fall.

I have not time to add more as I am surrounded with company to take leave of me. I retain an unalterable affection for you, which neither time or distance can change. My best love to Jack and Nelly, and regards to the rest of the Family, concludes me with the utmost truth and sincerity

Yr entire
G. Washington

Mt. Vernon

Philadelphia June 18. 1775.

My Dearest,

I am now set down to write
to you on a subject which fills me with inexpress-
ible concern — and this concern is greatly aggravated and increased when I reflect on the uneasiness I know it will give you — It has been determined in Congress, that the whole army raised
for the defence of the American Cause shall be put
put under my care, and that it is necessary
for me to proceed immediately to Boston to
take upon me the Command of it. — You may
believe me my dear Patcy, when I assure you
in the most solemn manner, that, so far from
seeking this appointment I have used every
endeavour in my power to avoid it, not only
from my unwillingness to part with you and
the Family, but from a consciousness of its
being a trust too great for my Capacity, and
that I should enjoy more real happiness and
felicity in one month with you, at home, than
I have the most distant prospect of reaping
abroad if my stay was to be seven times

THE CIVIL WAR

*This was never really contemplated in earnest.
I believe if either the North or the South had expected
their difficulties would result in this obstinate struggle,
the cold-blooded Puritan and the cock-witted Hugenot
and Cavalier would have made a compromise.*

GEORGE E. PICKETT

in a letter to his fiancée, June 27, 1862

Sullivan & Sarah

From Major Sullivan Ballou to Sarah Ballou

JULY 14TH 1861
CAMP CLARK WASHINGTON

My very dear Sarah

The indications are very strong that we shall move in a few days - perhaps tomorrow, Lest I should not be able to write you again, I feel impelled to write a few lines that may fall under your eye when I shall be no more. Our movement may be one of a few days duration and full of pleasure, and it may be one of severe conflict and death to me. "Not my will, but thine O God be done" If it is necessary that I should fall on the battle field for my country, I am ready. I have no misgivings about, or lack of courage confidence in the cause in which I am engaged, + my courage does not halt or falter. I know how strongly American civilations civilization now leans on the triumph of the government, + how great a debt we owe to those who went before us through the blood + sufferings of the Revolution, + I am willing, perfectly willing - to lay down all my joys in this life to help maintain this government + to pay that debt. But, my dear wife, when I know that with my own joys, I lay down nearly all of yours, + replace them in this life with cares + sorrows, when after having eaten for long years the bitter fruits of orphanage myself, I must offer it as the only sustenance to my dear little children. is it mean or dishonorable, that while the banner of my purpose floats calmly + proudly in the breeze, underneath, my unbounded love for you, my darling wife + children should struggle in fierce, though

HISTORICAL NOTE

Both the Confederate and Union soldiers, dressed in colorful new uniforms, were full of naive optimism when they met on the rolling field of Bull Run. Nearly nine hundred young men lost their lives on the fields of Matthews Hill, Henry Hill, and Chinn Ridge, and it became clear that the war's outcome would not be decided quickly. One year later, the war would again focus on Bull Run. This time the body count would reach 3,300.

useless contest with my love of Country. I cannot describe to you my feelings on this calm summer Sabbath night, when thousands now are sleeping around me, many of them enjoying, perhaps that last sleep before that of death, while I am suspicious that death is creeping around me with his fatal dart, as I sit communing with God, my Country and thee. I have sought most closely and diligently + often in my heart for a wrong motive in this hazarding the happiness of all those I love and I could find none. A pure love of my country and of the principles I have so often advocated before the people. Another name of honor that I love more than I fear death, has called upon me, + I have obeyed.

Sarah, my love for you is deathless; it seems to bind me with mightly cables that nothing but misfortune could break; and yet my love of country comes to me like a strong wind + bears me irresistably on with all those charms to the battle field. The memories of all the blissful moments I have spent with you come creeping over me, + I feel most grateful to God + to you that I have enjoyed them so long, and how hard it is for me to give them up + burn to ashes the hopes of future years. Where God willing, we might still have lived and loved together + seen our sons grow up to honorable manhood around us. I have, I know but few + small claims upon Divine Providence - but something whispers to me perhaps it is the wafted prayer of my little Edgar, that I shall return to my loved ones unharmed. If I do not, my dear Sarah never forget how much I loved you. And when my last breath escapes me - on the battle field - it will whisper your name. Forgive my many faults, and the many pains I have caused you. How thoughtless how foolish I have oftentimes been: How gladly I would wash out with my tears every little spot upon your happiness, + struggle with all

MAJOR SULLIVAN BALLOU, who volunteered to serve with the Second Regiment of Rhode Island's Volunteer Infantry, wrote this stirring letter on the night before leaving Washington for Manassas. Seven days after writing, on a Sunday morning, Ballou was wounded at the first battle of Bull Run. He died in a makeshift hospital at Sudley Church, Virginia, on July 26, 1861. His body was later exhumed and burned by Confederate soldiers. The following year his remains were personally retrieved by Governor William Sprague and interred in Providence. Ballou grew up with limited means, but became a Providence, Rhode Island, lawyer and served in the Rhode Island House of Representatives from 1853–55. He and the former Sarah Hart Shumway of Poughkeepsie, New York, had been married just six years when he died. Though Sullivan and Sarah had two children, Edgar and William, they have no living descendants.

During the the Persian Gulf War, servicemen sent copies of Ballou's letter home, choosing to let his heartfelt words do the talking for them. Junior high and high school English classes have studied the missive for its literary value.

Major Sulivan Ballou, 1860 engraving by J.A. O'Neill; Courtesy of the Rhode Island Historical Society

Sullivan & Sarah

the misfortunes of this world to shield you + your children from harm. But I cannot, I must watch you from the spirit land, and hover near you—while you buffet the storms with your precious fright, and wait with patience till we meet to part no more. But O Sarah, if the dead can come back to this Earth, + flit unseen around those they loved, I shall always be near you, In the gladdest of days, + in the darkest night, amidst your happiest scenes, and gloomiest hours, always - always, and if there be a soft breeze upon your cheek it shall be my breath; as the cool air fans your throbbing temples; it shall be my spirit passing by.

Sarah, do not mourn me dead, think I am gone and wait for thee, for we shall meet again, as for my little boys - they will grow up as I have done and never know a fathers love or care. Little Willie is too young to remember me long - and my blue eyed Edgar will keep my frolics with him among the dim memories of childhood.

Sarah, I have unbounded confidence in your maternal care, + your development of their characters, and feel that God will bless you in your holy work. Tell my two Mothers I call God's blessing upon them, O Sarah; come to me, and lead thither my children.

Sullivan

Robert & Mary

From Robert E. Lee
to Mary Custis Lee

JUNE 30, 1864

...Do you recollect what a happy day thirty-three years ago this was? How many hopes and pleasures it gave birth to. God has been very merciful and kind to us ... I pray that he may continue his mercy and blessings to us and give us a little peace and rest together in this world, and finally gather us and all he has given us around His throne in the world to come...

Robert E. Lee, though busy in the thick of battle as leader of the Confederate forces, took time to write wife Mary Custis Lee in commemoration of their thirty-third anniversary. Many of Lee's letters, however, took a more serious tone. From Richmond, on April 26, he wrote: *"I am very anxious about you. You will have to move and make arrangements to go to some point of safety which you must select. The Mount Vernon plate and pictures ought to be secured ...War is inevitable and there is no telling when it will burst around you."*

McLean House, Appomattox Courthouse, Virginia

He was the son of Revolutionary War hero "Light-Horse" Harry Lee, a friend of George Washington. She was the great-granddaughter of Washington's wife, an heiress of the Arlington estate across the Potomac from Washington. They were both Confederate heroes.

Granville & Annie

From George Granville Sharp to Anna Williamson Sharp

HOPKINSVILL KEN
APRILE 7TH 1865

Dear Annie

I have been going to write for several days but put it off till I heard from home again … I got two flowers to sen you one is a flowering ammon the other is a flowering quince The first ever I saw I got them the same place I got dinner Annie ant the news good richmond is doomed we had quite a time in town last night the houses wer illuminated and fires in the streets we shot thre rounds it was the first time I have shot my gun off Abbel was on picket and mist all the fun we would of had a good time if some of the boys had not got drank the officers got drunk first and I did not blame the boys so much there was non you know Co. C. Was the worst … There is talk that Johnson is making for kentucky and if he is he can easy take us in There is not more than 250 effective men here tho I think he wont get this far I was on picket night before last and it raind all night I stood from midnight till daylight it was the worst night I ever saw Annie I would like to see you all and ed and you the worst but I am well satisfied here and it begins to seem like home … Annie I want you to wite it dos me so much good to hear from you and edde I all ways wondered at soldiers wanting to hear from home but I know the reason now it is the love for the dear ones at home and known my wife and baby and father mother sisters and brother is deare to me than any thing but my country is at stake I must close dear you must write with love to all the folks and a differnt love for you and eddy as every your Husband

G G Sharp

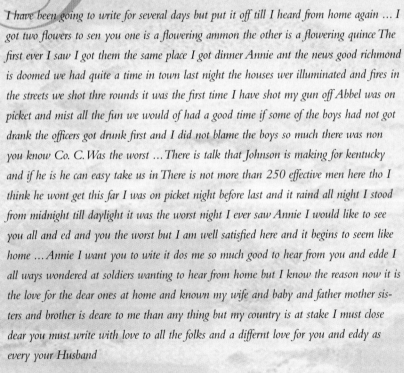

From George Granville Sharp to Anna Williamson Sharp

CAMP KENTUCKY MAY THE 3RD. 1865.

Dear Annie

…you speak of Lincoln murder and say you fear it will stop the progress for peace I do not think it will it has not stoped it so fare not one iota nor do I think it can for the rebs are playd out except in small sqads on this side of the missicippis river … Annie you dont know how bad I want to see you and our dear little baby he seems to me that he is the same litte babe he was when I kissed you and him and started I looked through the window and see you the last time but hope i can look through the window and see you with a look of joy on both of our faces before the summer is over … well Annie you sayd you wanted a long letter here it is but I fear it will not be interesting I must close with love to you and ed and to all my relations G G Sharp high Private

GEORGE GRANVILLE SHARP served in Company B of the 153rd Indiana Infantry with his brother Abel Lewis Sharp. Granville was twenty-two when he wrote these letters to wife Anna Williamson Sharp. Abel was married to Annie's sister, Sarah Louise Williamson. As Granville was a poor letter writer, Annie often learned of her husband's status through Sarah's letters from Abel. She often complained that he didn't write more.

Granville survived the Civil War, but in weakened health, according to his descendants. Living in the Huntington County area of Indiana, Granville and Annie had four more sons before he died of pneumonia at age fifty.

Granville & Annie

From Anna Williamson Sharp to George Granville Sharp

AT HOME SUNDAY MORNING JULY 9TH 1865

Dear Granville

I again take my pen in hand to let you know that we are all well and hope this will find you getting better … we Sent you nine dollars and my picture last Friday week I hope you have got them before this time I dont See why you do not get my letters better for I write So many but am getting pretty near out of heart writing I don't believe you begin to get half that I write I have only got fifteen letters from you Since you went away the last time and Sarah has got fifty four from Abel … I try to keep in good heart I am in hopes you think of me and Eddie often if you dont write he is Sitting in his wagon now playing with a Straw well Granvill I dont know hardly what I write that will interest you … I am looking for you all the time and I am in hopes I wont look in vain I want you to write often and not wait for a letter every time I am as ever your loving wife

Annie

HISTORICAL NOTE

Though there were few trained soldiers in Indiana at the onset of the Civil War, thousands of volunteers assembled in Indianapolis within a week of the assault on Fort Sumter. Within a year, more than 61,000 Indiana men enlisted. By war's end, a total of 196,000 Union soldiers had been provided by Indiana. There were 7,243 Hoosiers killed or mortally wounded during the war; 17,500 perished of disease or accidents.

THE SPANISH-AMERICAN WAR

What kind of shoes
Do the rough riders wear?
Buttons on the side,
Cost five and a half a pair
It was all about that Battleship of Maine

AMERICAN FOLK SONG OF THE
SPANISH-AMERICAN WAR PERIOD

Roy & Margaret

From Roy Campbell Smith
to Margaret Sampson Smith

DRY TORTUGAS
U.S.S. *INDIANA*
10 MARCH 1898

Your sweet letter of the 4th was the part of the "Porter's" arrival that gave me the most satisfaction. I knew that your spirit was such that you would have no fight for our rights - even if you had several fathers, husbands and sons all engaged. And as your Mother was able to go through the trial bravely, I am sure you have more than imbibed all her spirit.

Do not assume that I have any fears about the other matter. Whatever else you are, you are not vain. You are a great deal more attractive than you have any idea of. I have never attached the least blame to your actions, but people who are not vain often do not realize what motives may be ascribed to them. If I have made my meaning clear, I am perfectly willing to leave to your judgment your entire future course. I have in you the most complete confidence. What you have found in me to be devoted to I do not know, except that women will love without the least reason; and if I wanted any more proofs of your affection than you have already given me a thousand times, I should simply be intolerable…

Yours,
Roy

16 MARCH 1898

…we had another torpedo-boat attack last night, but the boats were routed…I take it my M.R. policy is of no use except for death from natural causes. Death from wounds secures the return of premiums only…I cannot make any more guesses on old newspaper news. Do not be worried till war actually begins, as Spain may back down at any time…

18 March 1898

...I am sorry to hear of Marjorie's mumps by your letter of the 14th. There is lots of trouble, isn't there?...

3 April 1898

...I hope you had a good time at the Wells' party. I am glad you find some little enjoyment occasionally and do not have all work and worry, such as care of sick children and the like...Do you feel like dancing at dinner parties?...

...We loaded our big guns this evening for the first time with the hope that we should not have to back the shells out from the muzzle...

Off Key West
6 April 1898

...Why do you not make any comment on what I do write? "I received your letter of the 10th," for instance, does not convey anything, as I can have no idea by that time what was in my letter of the 10th...

24 April 1898 [The day Spain declared war]

Dear Margaret,
We were rather caught on our last Tortugas trip, as we had to start for war minus washed clothes, provisions and mail. However with "Patience and Cheerfulness" as a motto we hope to come out all right...

MARGARET ALDRICH SAMPSON, the daughter of a Rear Admiral William T. Sampson, probably knew what she was getting into when she married Naval Academy graduate Roy Campbell Smith. His fifty-five-year navy career took him around the world, on more than a dozen warships, and into the role of teacher, author, and even governor of Guam during World War I. Captain Smith was awarded the Navy Cross, the Victory Medal, the Sampson Medal, the Spanish Campaign Medal, and the Mexican Service Medal. The couple had two sons and a daughter.

6 March 1898

Roy&Margaret

27 APRIL 1898

...Do you not think the war is a just one? The simplest view to me is that our tranquillity had been too long disturbed, and that the culmination in the "Maine" disaster proved Spain's incompetence; therefore we were entirely justified in saying "You must move away now, we have stood you as long as we can..."

...tell Campbell I enjoyed his letter. We shall have to see about the pup when I get home (He wanted $25. Don't tell him I said so.) He is a little too young to be Jack-of-the-Dust, and his mother could not afford to have all the men in the family in the war. I hope his thumb is better. Incidentally, you might tell both the children sometime, not now, not to ask for presents in their letters.

I am sorry Marjorie takes the war so hard. Tell her I expect to come back all right after it is all over, and then she will be glad I was in it...

...Please do not write me about these parties that you go to because you are so blue. If you are blue on my account I do not want anyone else to cheer you up...

30 APRIL 1898

...I am glad you are able to feel calm. The danger is really not as great as most people imagine. Some people will probably get hurt, but the percentage of deaths in a naval war is not normally great. Your address is at the Department, and should anything be known there of sufficient interest concerning me, you will be informed...

BATTLESHIP INDIANA

Dry Tortugas,
10 March, 1898.

Dear Margaret,

It is time to begin another letter, to be forwarded when opportunity offers. I hope there will be more opportunities in future, for Capt. Philip protested against three battleships being left over . . . . . without communi . . . . any sh . . . broken . . . a wee . . .

WORLD WAR I

We often write to mothers, to sweethearts and to wives,
And tell how those who loved them have given up their lives;
If we're not always truthful, our lies are always kind,
Our letters lie to cheer them, to solace and to cheer them,
Oh: anything to cheer them, — the women left behind.

PATRICK MACGILL
Vermelles, August 1915

Postcards from the front

P aper was in short supply during World War I—and highly impractical in the trenches. So soldiers took advantage of their free time to buy postcards. Many were adorned with themes of love, helpful for those less than able with a pen. Other cards were intricately hand stitched by local refugees trying to profit from the newcomers. It was popular to have special photos made into postcards to reassure those back home that all was well.

Telling "Chateau Thierry" or "In Love and War"

A Red Cross nurse in love with a wounded U.S. soldier billeted at a farmhouse back of the firing line in France. At a glance the scene appears commonplace, but by observing closely, a remarkable likeness of the two printed words "Love" and "War" is impressed upon the mind.

FROM MOVIE MOSS - CO. L. 10. INF.
CAMP E.S. OTIS
CANAL. ZONE. PANAMA.

Miss Lillian my Dear girl I will now send you one of my picture. though it doesn't mount to very much. I was out in the woods. now you must send me yours now. as Ever Yours.

By. By. Love.

CARD

U.S. POSTAGE
2 CENTS

THIS SPACE FOR ADDRESS ONLY

Miss. Margarett Boyles
247 Liberty St.
Martinsburg
W Va.

NEWLY ENLISTED CAVALRYMAN HOW

THIS SPACE FOR WRITING MESSAGE

EDWARD '35

OCT 14
5-PM
1917

U.S. ARMY SERIES 26

I'll always think
of you

Clay & his wife

Private Clay T. Hayden
to his wife

CAMP SHERMAN
5-14-18

My Darling Wife

Just a few lines to let you know that I am still among the living

Just came in from the Rifle Range today was out there seven days

Just a little idea of the trip the Range is five miles from Camp Sherman and we walked out and back and had to carry out equipment which weighs 60 lbs that was what we had in our packs and had to cary rifle also which weighs 9 lbs and we was camped in a corn field and had to sleep on the ground and it rained about every day that we was out some trip sure never had my clothes on for seven days and never washed but once and that was in a pond after it had rained all night. they only would let us have one quart of watter a day and believe me after the first day everyone sure did use water very careful they had to haul all the watter wouldn't use any well watter at all just a quart of watter for me is not very much but I got along alright. would tell you more but I am in the army now

Oh yes, Recd a letter to night that was written May 3 and I also recd a letter last eve out at the Range that was wrote after the one on May 3 my mail has been all bawled up all of the boys have been kicking one guy Recd seven letters Last Eve.

well Dear you ask me about buying a Car well if I was going to buy I would buy a Dodge $785 five passenger they are not any more expensive than a ford and I like them much better

now about you going to work I think you had better go up and spend a couple of months with Mother + Dad you never had a real vacation so you had better take one now while you can Dear I think you can get along alright with the interest and what the Government will pay you that will be $30 Per month have you ever recd any Insurance

HISTORICAL NOTE

Named for Civil War General William Tecumseh Sherman, Camp Sherman was garrisoned in spring 1917 in South Central Ohio. The post was abandoned in 1921.

Founded in 1844, the YMCA, or Young Men's Christian Association, operated service clubs for military personnel during both world wars.

Policy from the Government I had them all mailed to you but it takes them a long while to get 40,000 mailed out

well Dearest you ask me if I wanted my underwere don't send them I have more then I can take care of now but would like to have about six Khaka handkerchief

well Dear this is all I have time to write so will say Bye Bye Darling

oh yes I need a recd a letter from Melda + also one from Lena

a thousand Big sweet Kisses
Clay
Co H. 332 Inf
Sec a. 24.
Camp Sherman

P.S. we start out on a 40 mile Hike in the morning we get up at 4 a.m.

CAMP SHERMAN, OHIO [POSTMARKED THREE DAYS LATER]

My Darling wife

Recd your most welcome letter Recd it the same Eve that I mailed your letter sure was glad to hear from you. I think that I have Received all your letters now

I get my mail every Eve when I am in Camp well we didn't go on the 40 mile hike we have been taking Gas mask Instructions since we came back from the Range we work every minute in the day

when you write to Melda tell her that I Recd her letter and I appreciated it very much but I am so busy that I haven't ans yet

I am sleeping in a tent and we don't have any light so you see I can't write very well after I get through work and when you write to Lena tell her the same as Melda but I sure do think of you Darling every minute

I could just _love_ _you_ to pieces if you was here well Darling we sure did enjoy our selves for a couple of months didn't we well they are not giveing _any one_ a furlough now we have to work every Sunday thats going some but will be here home just as soon as I can get a furlough sure would like to see you but it will be pretty hard for me to see any one here for a while we are getting the same training in four weeks as the other boys got in seven months

so we are very busy will have to close as it is dark. Bye Bye Clay

Roy & C. B. & Martha

Two letters to Martha Perkins

FEB. 1, 1920

My dear Miss Perkins!

Hello, <u>good</u>, night, nurse! I shall never forget the careful administration of those cooling and soothing lotions that were so welcome to my eyes those first few nights of my first hospital experience. You no doubt realize the great relief that you rendered to us fellows, but, you cannot begin to know how thankful we all were and ever will be for the faithful care. After it was over and we were back again in the fight I have heard the fellows speak about it many times. I thank you most sincerely. We were all very much disappointed that we were unable to see. However, after being in Base #32 for two or three weeks we could see some...

Do you remember Sergt. Hershman and Pvt. Warren both of them were gassed and there in the hospital when I was there? We lost them both in the Argonne. We were advancing in the rain the 30th of Sept. or 1st of Oct. when a gas shell exploded hitting them and inflicting mortal wounds as well as gassing them with mustard again from which both died that night. We lost several men after that from shell fire and all had very close calls... Some of the boys were never able to reenter the fray after their first gas. A friend of mine still has a cough from it and another has lost a lung as a result of fosgine [phosgene] gas received the night we entered the Argonne above Florent.

As for me I feel about as robust as ever. I managed to wheeze along and work the stuff out of my system after getting thru three weeks of the replacement camp drill at Lefoil la Grande. From there to Chaumont, to Is-sur-Tiel, to Chatteau-Thierry, to Fere-en Tordnois and ville-en-Tordnois and thence to College Point Woods where I met my good old Capt Hubbell... It seemed like getting back home, <u>almost</u> . This was Aug. 25 just two months after the gassing.

HISTORICAL NOTE

At the declaration of World War I in 1917, there were 403 nurses on active duty in twelve hospitals. By November 11, 1918, there were 21,480.

Like the Finance Corps or the Military Police Corps, the Army Nurse Corps is today one of seventeen combat service support arms of the U.S. Army.

When the armistice came we were up on the Meuse river at Reuelly. From there we hiked 150 miles back to La Terte-sul-Aube near Chaumont from Nov. 13 to Dec. 5th. We were enroute about 14 days. In that time we slept in old prison camps in the ground and everywhere so that we were covered with vermin. It was worse than fighting, making that trip.

Well, its over now and we're back here at the old stand selling knowledge in the halls of Minerva. I am instructor in Am. History and Civics to a hundred ten H.S. juniors and seniors. It is some job too, but I manage to pay my board and lodging and buy postage.

When you're not overworked I'd be delighted to hear from you about your experiences "over there" and "over here." Don't forget that I haven't see you yet and would like to. You have that on me.

Yours very truly,
L. Roy Quick

———— ◆◆◆◆ ————

PARIS, FRANCE
OCT. 21, 1918

My Dear Miss Perkins,
Just a word to thank you for your kindness to me while I was in the hospital. I want you to know that the boys appreciate what you girls are doing. When the war is over and the medals are passed around I trust the Red Cross nurses will not be forgotten. Medals or no medals, the boys will not forget those who cared for them—even though the ailment, as in my case, might have been "petite." Any time I may be of any service to you, or any of the boys in Hut 6, do not hesitate to call on me.

Sincerely,
C. B. Scott, Sgt. 1st Class
APO 702
c/o D.I.M.

War love letters weren't just written during wars. Martha Perkins, like many Red Cross and Army Nurse Corps nurses who tended to men in their hour of need, was the object of much admiration from those she treated. She was an adventuresome young woman who left her Pomfret, Vermont, home for nursing school as soon as war broke out in Europe. She became a Red Cross nurse at age twenty-six; two months later she joined the army.

In May 1918, Martha arrived at Evacuation Hospital No. 2 in Baccarat, France, just as the hospital moved closer to the lines. She wrote home that they had frequent air raids, blackouts, and shells whizzing overhead looking for the nearby ammunition dump: "We have to feed our patients onions to find them in the dark."

In October 1918, Martha wrote of "much influenza" at Camp Hospital No. 4, outside Paris. Indeed, an influenza epidemic had begun in September of that year and would claim the lives of more than two hundred nurses. No nurses were reported to have died as a result of enemy action. Martha's boss, Beatrice M. MacDonald, was the first of three winners of the Distinguished Service Cross for rendering aid in combat.

Martha corresponded regularly with her parents throughout her adventures in Europe. She never, however, wrote of romance. Perhaps it was not to offend her parents' sensibilities, or perhaps she was keenly aware of the sensors scrutinizing all mail. It is not known how much attention she paid to potential suitors like L. Roy Quick and C. B. Scott.

Josiah & his mother

From Josiah P. Rowe Jr. to his mother

CAMPO D'AVIAZIONE, SUD
FOGGIA, ITALY
JANUARY 28, 1918

...Although most of us have passed that happy period and the innocent pleasures of childhood will not come again, one can never grow so old as not to feel the spell of youthful joys and we will all be kids again when we get back together. That sounds like I am a million years old, doesn't it?...

MARCH 2, 1918

I can't help from smiling in sweet satisfaction and smacking my lips with ecstatic bliss at every thought of the rapturous hours spent in riotous living immediately after the receipt of the long-looked-for box on Saturday, February 24. Such tasty

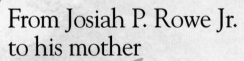

morsels of such delicate food have never caused more genuine joy and happiness in the heart of man before. Mother dear, I can never thank you and others in proportion with what you deserve for sending me such a nice, large box of so many good things, but let it be known that I deeply appreciate it all not only for the thoughtfulness which it represented, but also because of the aching void which was filled and the pangs of hunger which were appeased... I shared things with some other boys in return for some bits from their boxes, but believe me I defended that fruit cake with my life and stretched it out over two days of blissful contentment...

1st Lt. Josiah P. Rowe, Jr.

HISTORICAL NOTE

Of the 11,000 pilots trained by the U.S. Army, just over one-third were to get to Europe before the end of the war. Of these, only about six hundred—including Josiah P. Rowe Jr.—saw combat.

MARCH 24, 1918

…Rome is surely a great place and I want to go back before I leave Italy. One important feature that must not be overlooked is the great improvement over other places in the way of girls. There were lots of pretty girls, well dressed and comely, and to show that we haven't forgotten all about our girls at home, we took a second look at all these so as to be better able to compare them with the standard of the world…

AVIATION CORPS IN ITALY
8TH AVIATION INSTRUCTION CENTER
AMERICAN EXPEDITIONARY FORCES
MAY 14, 1918

…About 10 o'clock we coupled up and went for a walk in the moonlight. I drew the Italian girl …You know, in the better families in Italy a couple is never without a chaperone until after the marriage. The Italians must have a lot of fun making love to a girl with an old-maid chaperone sitting on the other end of the sofa. It's a mystery to me how they ever get married over here. I still feel highly flattered that her aunt decided to stay in that night…
I don't remember ever having been with a girl who had never been out before and I didn't know what in the dickens was expected of a fellow in Italy. I certainly could not feel at ease when I knew that all mankind and Americans in particular were being judged by me.
… She said that she had always wanted to go to Nebraska to see the great fields of wheat, but I told her they were no different from the fields of gently swaying spaghetti … She is a mighty nice little girl but don't be looking for me to bring her home as a souvenir.

JUNE 2, 1918

My dearest Mother:
…I have just received your letter written on Mother's Day, which made me feel both good and bad. I appreciate your kind thoughts, but it hurts me to think that the occasion came and went without my writing to you. Unfortunately we knew nothing about it until two weeks after it passed. But every day is Mother's Day with me now. Maybe it didn't used to be, but not a day goes by now that I don't think of you and when I get back I will do something besides think. So long; love to all.

Devotedly,
Josiah

A most pervasive kind of love letter, during every war, was written from son to mother. Josiah P. Rowe Jr. wrote his mother and family at least once a month during his service in World War I. He vividly, and quite candidly, described experiences ranging from his first solo flight to his first date with an Italian girl. Rowe's prowess as a writer was evident early on.

Rowe was sent overseas with the United States Air Service of the American Expeditionary Forces in October 1917. After several rounds of flight training, he joined the 147th Aero Squadron, First Pursuit Group, in Rembercourt where he flew combat patrols until the end of the war. His love of flying continued, and eventually he owned his own plane.

Rowe would later become editor and publisher of *The Free Lance-Star*, the daily newspaper in his native Fredericksburg, Virginia. And, like his father and grandfather before him and his son Josiah after, Rowe also served as mayor of Fredericksburg. Upon his death in 1949, his sons succeeded him as joint publishers of the successful newspaper.

WORLD WAR II

...Letters are the only real contact with home. I guess I could forget I had a home, or dear ones in the Old Country, if it weren't for mail, not to mention the fact that I would have a real attack of the blues...

LIEUTENANT (JUNIOR GRADE) RALPH M. ATHERTON, USNR
June 27, 1945

We are now in this war. We are all in it—all the way. Every single man, woman, and child is a partner in the most tremendous undertaking of our American history. We must share together the bad news and the good news, the defeats and the victories—the changing fortunes of war.

President FRANKLIN D. ROOSEVELT, in a fireside radio chat delivered on December 9, 1941, two days after Japan attacked Pearl Harbor and two days before the United States formally entered the war against Germany and Italy.

Sam & Barbara

From Sam Head to Barbara Head

NAVAL HOSPITAL
DECEMBER 19, 41

Hello Honey

Well here I am writing another letter without even getting a single one from you. But you see I haven't been over to the barracks since I come to the hospital. So I guess all of my mail is over there. They wouldn't bother themselves about sending the mail over here to me. I take it for granted that you did write didn't you? I expect to get out of here about Friday morning.

Well! We are having a little excitement now. I didn't think the . . . [Japanese] would even try a thing like that so we are going to have to lower the boom on them . . . Anyway, I don't know where I will be sent. I put in to go to sea but you can never tell where a person will be sent. There sure is a lot of things here in Washington. I can look out the window here and see the White House. there are so many cars around there, that it is almost impossible to walk down there. Sure was a crowd here yesterday when the president declared war . . .

Gee Barbara I had the sweetest dream about you the other night. If I was there I could really tell you what we did and where we went. I thought we were at sea on a ship. Funny thing's I didn't dream about a nice moonlight night. I thougt it was raining + cold but I know we would enjoy that if only we were together. I know I would.

There are a lot of news coming over the radio but don't believe the radio + those damn newspapers. No one will ever know just what we are doing. And that can't be made public. You know we are ordered not to give out any info at all. We will kick the hell out of those . . . [Japanese] yet. You know the battle ship which was sunk? Well I used to do duty on it. I knew all the Marines aboard it. Sure was bad.

Guess I had better close. Sure looks as though it was going to snow here. Answer soon Honey cause I want to hear from you. Lots of love, Sam

HISTORICAL NOTE

The assault on Iwo Jima cost the Marine Corps about twenty-five thousand casualties, more than any other engagement in the corps's history.

29 DEC. 44
PACIFIC AREA

Dearest Darling Wife:

…You and the kids are all I worry + would do anything in the whole world for. As I have told you before darling we will live in a little world of our own when I do get back. I am glad everything was fixed for the kids at Xmas. I would have loved to more than anything in the world, besides being there, to have bought gifts for all of you. But it is almost an impossible thing to do over here sugar. I am sure you will understand. I will make up for it next time darling…

Now about the house you were talking about. I wish you would wait a few more months before you did make a decision. You see dear, it is just about time for this war to start to an end + you know how all messed up things will be. In other words dear I just cannot tell you in this letter why I want you to wait a couple of months, but try to put two + two together…

Well dear I must close as it is about taps. I wish you were here tonite. We have a full moon. Sure is a pretty scene here. Reminds me of the time we rode around Lake Tahoma at night and parked. Remember? I love you dear + think you are wonderful. Good night + give the kids my love.

Love always,
Sam

SAM HEAD and Barbara Austin grew up next door to each other in Marion, North Carolina. Thanksgiving at Sam's house in 1941 was their first date. Four months later they married. She was seventeen. He was twenty, and on leave.

Sam Head didn't want his young wife to make any big financial decisions because he knew he was headed for a confrontation at Iwo Jima. His second day on the island, a shell exploded in his foxhole, tearing into his leg and killing the friend next to him.

After two decades with the Marine Corps, Captain Sam Head retired in 1960. He and Barbara, now of Macon, Georgia, celebrated their fifty-fifth anniversary in 1997. One of their two daughters and a grandson have made Marine Corps service a three-generation family tradition. Sam still has shrapnel in his leg.

Robert&Margaret

From Robert H. Loring
to Margaret Ann Binford Loring

JUNG HOTEL, NEW ORLEANS
MARCH 1943 FRIDAY 11:00

My dearest Darling:

Here I sit with two bottles of beer waiting for you. What <u>can't</u> it be 7:45 tomorrow instead of just 11:00 tonight? And why do we ever have to be separated? It just isn't right, that's all.

I feel the sort of funny feeling that this is <u>to</u> you—the Post Office Dept. won't be coming between us on this.

I've just been thinking of the number of nights I've spent like this before and after our marriage—just sitting and wishing <u>you</u> were with me. So many times when I was out with the "boys" or on a trip <u>supposedly</u> raising hell—so many times I have spent it just like this—all by myself and eating my heart out for you.

You know we both have too much pride, or something. I've never had the guts to tell you that before—but a lot of my "good times" that I've come home and "blowed off" about were just like this—a dismal empty "wanting you" feeling.

Oh, there are so many things I've never told you and want to—so much. Why can't we let our hair down from now on and just love each other with no stops—with no intermissions—and with absolutely no regard for whatever the future may bring! Our time—even though a life time—is so very very short.

I can't put it in words, but I worship you. The very happiest moments of my life have been with you. My most exciting anticipations have been the thoughts of getting home to you.

Of course, I always breezed in with a very nonchalant air. Darling, believe me, it was just to cover up the throbbing of my heart and the—if you will—excruciating joy of my soul at the sight of you.

You are the Alpha and Omega to me. You anti-date my very birth and post date my death.

Why I've been too stubborn to <u>constantly</u> let you know all this I <u>don't</u> know. I have evaded this issue a 1001 <u>little</u> ways by trying to show you in one way or another, but I'm afraid I've never faced it bravely.

When I used to come from the torture of a drill field to you in Baltimore I would let *down.* Let *down, mind you, when the only thing that had brought me through the day was the reward of seeing you that night. Why didn't I let you know that? I think perhaps you* did *know, but it was mighty selfish of me just to take it for granted.*

This is silly—and I'll destroy this letter—as I've done others to you, but—oh, no I won't. That's just my point.

New Orleans is a city for love. You can just see it on the street. Let's make it just that for us. Let's forget our puritan backgrounds and just be mighty honest with each other. Let's make up for lost time—let's make up for any future time we'll be separated.

Darling, I've missed you so much. I've needed you a thousand times. Just to have you grab me by the hand crossing a street would have done wonders for me. Just to have had you cuddle at night would have made everything all right.

I'm a baby about you, I'm afraid. But you're the one *thing in the world more important to me than* I *am. The thought of an enemy submarine don't bother me nearly so much as the thoughts of a day without you. I love you, my own Darling, and always will—more and more every day.*

Sincerely and with all my love and affection

Your husband

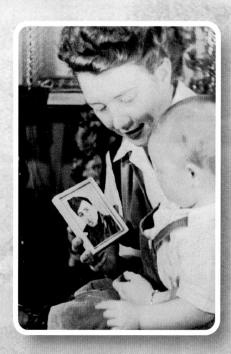

Indiana native Robert H. Loring wrote to Margaret, his wife of two years, on hotel stationery. It was a matter of hours before she joined him. Days later, he was shipped out to the European theater of operations in England to eventually serve among the follow-up troops that landed at Normandy two weeks after D-Day. His unit then joined Patton's Third Army in the race across France.

From Robert H. Loring to his one-year-old son, Robert B. Loring

18 JANUARY 1945

Dear Son:

Judging from everything I have heard about you, it is obvious that you are a most precocious young man; however, I seriously doubt if you have learned to read by this time. For that reason it may be a bit unusual for me to be writing to you tonight, but it's your first birthday, and we can't afford to let that pass totally unobserved. Perhaps the main reason I'm writing you, though, is to give me the very selfish pleasure of writing the two words "Dear son"—just so I could see how they look on paper and how it would feel for me to write them.

First of all, let me tell you that I'm not going to bore you with a lot of sob-sister stuff about how much I want to see you, how often I've said "Dear Son" softly to myself, and how often I have thought of you. Those things just go without saying, and you and I can dispense with any tear-jerking phrases.

Scientists and psychologists are not in total agreement about just how much comprehension and logical reasoning is present in a mind which has reached the ripe old age of one year. However, from the things that have been written me about you, my guess is

Robert & Margaret & their son

Margaret and Robert's son, Robert B. Loring, was conceived during their rendezvous in New Orleans—he was born nine months later. He didn't meet his father until December 1945.

Robert Loring returned safely home. The family moved to Miami, where Robert embraced a career teaching high school and even served as president of the Florida Classroom Teachers Association. He suffered a stroke and died in 1965.

When Margaret Loring died in 1986, her son found his father's letter to her pressed between this prewar picture of the couple and its frame. He believes that his mother probably hid it there to keep her husband from throwing it away. In all, the senior Loring wrote 450 letters to his wife during his training and World War II service.

that you in your own way have a pretty good idea of what's going on in this world today, and like everyone else you are doing all that you can to help out. For example, I feel sure that you have sensed that this has been a tough year for your mother, and you have been doing your very best to help cheer her up in as many ways as you can.

Every little bit of affection that you show her and every single laugh she has with you comes along straight to me through the mail. So, you see that it is no exaggeration when I tell you that you have done a fine morale building job over here as well as on the homefront.

Your mother—and I know you have already discovered this for yourself—your mother is the finest person in all this world. We are both mighty fortunate to have her, and we must never forget that. Her happiness must always come first to us; and you have already demonstrated that you in your own way understand that. Bob, if ever an angel walked this earth among us mortals, I believe that angel is your mother. I needn't tell you any more than that, but you and I must always exert our very best efforts to be worthy of her.

There is a great deal I could write you about this war. Fifteen years from now you will be studying the war in your high school Sophomore history course, and perhaps I can give you a few pointers that will help at that time. Too often we dismiss a war in history as a certain number of meaningless dates to be remembered along with the names of General-So-and-so and what happened to a couple of countries.

When the time comes, I'll want you to know a lot more about this war than that; I'll want you to see it clearly in its true light—a colossal collection of all the greatest tragedies this world has ever known. I'll want you to know not only what happened to a couple of countries, but I'll want you to know what happened to the people of those countries. For example, Bob, tonight all over this world there are many boys who are just one year old, like you, but differ from you because they will never recover from the effects of this war. Some of those one year old boys have actually lost their lives in this war after having had them for such a short time; some of them have lost their parents and their homes; and some of them are destined to go through life crippled and diseased only because it was their misfortune to have been born in one of these many war torn countries.

Tonight as you are having your first birthday, I'm thinking of you, naturally, but somehow I can't forget those other boys your age. You can understand why I can safely say to you that you were born in the greatest country of them all. For that reason it will be necessary for your country as well as your generation to take the lead in helping to rebuild and repair this world in the years to come.

While you are helping the people of these other nations in the future, perhaps you will be able to teach them a certain fundamental truth. If you can only show them that it is better to save a life than to take one; if you can convince them that it is far greater to build than to destroy; if by your example you can teach them that it is more pleasurable to give than to rob, then you and your kind will have accomplished something that no other generation has. If all of you who are one year old tonight could somehow dedicate yourselves to that single and simple premise, then together you would have succeeded in outlawing the tragedy of war for all time to come.

Yes, there are many, many things I could write you about tonight, but that can all wait till I see you. The important thing is that it's your first birthday. I know you have everything you want and need right now; you are surrounded by the love and affection of your mother and two sets of mighty fine grandparents. You are with those who love you and want you and that is important.

It's not the normal thing for a red-blooded, wide awake boy like you to have to do without having his father fussing about him. Perhaps in your own way you are even missing me a little bit and wondering why I'm not with you where I should be. Well, Bob, that's just another one of the tragedies of this war; but when you consider these other one year old boys that I have already written you about, you will agree with me that ours is only a minor tragedy by comparison.

There's nothing in this world that I wouldn't give to be with you and your mother tonight; I felt that same way when your first Christmas passed by us, and I've felt just like that every day and every night since your mother went down into the valley of the shadow of death to bring you home to us a year ago today. But you can see, and you must understand, that you and I are only giving up a little of our time together for the same reason that many fathers and many sons have given up their lives. They didn't complain, so we won't. Rather we must be thankful that the sacrifice that we have been called on to make has been so very small.

I have your most recent picture here in front of me—you are a fine looking boy, and I'm proud of you. You have a good name, and you were born on the right side of the tracks. You are starting the race even with the rest and there is no handicap; the finish line is up to you. Over here we are all hoping that the track will be in better shape for you; I guess that's why we are all here.

Happy first birthday to you, Son. May God bless you and guide you and the others your age as you all proceed from here on to the Future.

Sincerely,
Your Dad

Raymond & Margaret

From Admiral Raymond A. Spruance to Margaret Dean Spruance

U.S.S. *NORTHHAMPTON*
FEBRUARY 7, 1942

...I don't believe that I am going to enjoy the beauties of this part of the world, nor the war either, nearly as much without you...Please write fully and regularly. Get those tires retreaded. Much love to you both. Life has certainly lost its interest for me since you left, and the worst of it is that I have no definite date to look forward to when I shall see you again.

Raymond

JULY 4, 1943

...Yesterday was my 57th birthday and the day before my 40th anniversary of entering the Naval Academy. This leaves only seven years before I have to go on the shelf, and then you and I can start out to see those parts of the world that are still intact and open to visitors...

MARCH 13, 1945

...A couple of days ago I sent you rolled up in a mailing tube the finest photograph this war has given us up-to-date. It is the Marines raising the U.S. flag on top of Suribachi. When we settle down, I want to have this picture framed. Some first class sculptor should do this in bronze, it is so perfect...

ADMIRAL RAYMOND A. SPRUANCE was a warrior, strategist, tactician, and frequent letter-writer. But the man who turned the tide for the U.S. forces at the battle of Midway Island concentrated on far more practical matters than romance when writing home. Many women took on new responsibilities while their husbands fought the war, and Margaret Spruance was no exception. She filed income taxes for the first time and took care of car maintenance with the help of her husband's missives.

Spruance's letters didn't mention his activities as commander of Cruiser Division Five of the Pacific Fleet or as Admiral Chester W. Nimitz's chief of staff. He was promoted to admiral at age fifty-seven, the youngest at that time.

Just after the war, Spruance relieved Nimitz as Commander in Chief of the Pacific Fleet, a position he held for a mere ten weeks before being assigned as president of the Naval War College in Newport, Rhode Island. He retired twice, once interrupted by his appointment as ambassador to the Phillipines, and died in 1969. Spruance is buried in San Francisco next to his old comrade in arms, Chester Nimitz.

The picture Spruance wrote home about has become one of the best-known images of any war. Mount Suribachi fell to the Twenty-eighth Marines on February 23. The photo, however, actually depicted a second flag-raising. The battalion commander wanted to save the historic, first flag, so he ordered another one raised. Associated Press photographer Joe Rosenthal captured the second flag-raising. The image was indeed sculpted, in bronze, into the stunning Iwo Jima Marine Corps Memorial near Arlington National Cemetery.

Frances & the General

From Frances Newman
to Major General C. B. Cates

ROBINS FIELD, GEORGIA
24 APRIL 1945.

COMMANDING GENERAL,
FOURTH MARINE DIVISION,
C/O FLEET POST OFFICE,
SAN FRANCISCO, CALIFORNIA.

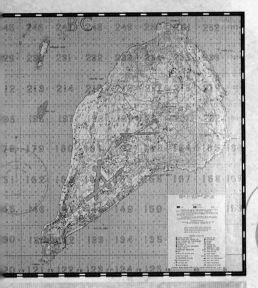

HISTORICAL NOTE

Iwo Jima, the largest of the three Volcano Islands in the Western Pacific, was invaded by U.S. Marines February 19, 1945, and conquered March 16 after fierce fighting. Sergeant James R. Newman was among 4,189 United States Marines killed at Iwo Jima. The U.S. also suffered 15,308 wounded and 441 missing, while Japanese losses were 22,000 killed and captured. Iwo Jima was returned to Japan in 1968.

Dear Sir:

On February 23rd, 1945, my only brother, Sgt. James R. Newman, USMCR, died on Iwo Jima. The telegram from the War Department came to us on March 29th.

Of course you did not know Bob personally. To you he was just another one of your men to help carry on the fighting Marine tradition. But to us, he was everything. I know that thousands of others just as dear died over there. It was a great battle and cost many thousands of lives. Bob loved the Marines so much and since he had to die, I find comfort in the fact that he was with the outfit that he loved most. He always wanted a Marine dress uniform and the "Marine Hymn" was his favorite song so I like to think of him as in the last two lines, "They will find the streets are guarded by the United States Marines." He was such a darling.

We miss him so much and the future is going to be unbearably empty without him, but I know he wouldn't want us to brood or grieve over him so I'm trying to carry on as usual. The last thing he ever said when he boarded the bus and headed for boot camp almost two years agao was, "Keep your chin up." It's been up ever since then and it's staying up. It almost dropped when we heard of this death, but I know he'd want me to be a soldier and in my small way, to carry on for him. So that is why, as a civilian warworker on an Army Air Field (I work in the Classification and Assignment Office where a majority of the Form 20's of Robins Field are maintained) I am doing my very best. Through our Office each day come the men reporting on the Field. When these boys first arrive here, they are bewildered and blue, they want places for their familiy and many other things. Though it is not a part of my job, I like to help those boys all I can by finding them places for their families and the other little things that one can do to make their lives a little easier. I used to do it for Bob, now I still do it in his memory for I know that someone was there to help him when he needed it most. I can not say that I am glad we had him to give for our Country, for I'm not. Sometimes I wonder if it is worth the sacrifice the boys are making. But if this is a better world for the sacrifice that they made, they will not have died in vain.

I know Bob is dead, but yet I can not believe it. To me he will never die. He will be the same happy, carefree curly-haired boy he was when he left.

I have written to one of his best friends for over a year. I have been expecting a letter from him ever since we got the telegram but I still haven't heard anything. I do not know his home address (all I know is that he is from Jackson, Mississippi) but I would like very much to know whether or not he is still alive. And also his Lieutenant. He never told us his name, but in almost every letter, he told us how lucky he was in having such a wonderful Lieutenant. I would like very much to know whether especially they, and also the other members of his team are still alive. He told us so much about them that I almost feel as if I know them personally. Even though I have lost the deepest interest in the Marine Corps to me, I would like to know the progress of the Team since he loved it so much, and maybe I would be able to send them things in his memory. If I could help them in some way, I would also be helping him.

I recently met a Marine who told me that you were one of the finest people he had ever known and he knew that if I wrote to you that you would give me information that I wanted. I hope that Bob didn't have to suffer. He was so young to be hurt.

My heart is still there with the Fourth Marine division and will always be. I love the Marines, every though they took all that I hold dear. But there are thousands of other homes just as we are.

I would appreciate it more than you will every know if you will try to locate Team 3.2 for me.

May God Bless you sir, as you lead those fine boys into battle and grant that this may soon be over, and all the boys can come home

GENERAL CLIFTON B. CATES did much more than respond with a letter to Frances Newman's heartfelt missive. He sent a corsage of white orchids for her eighteenth birthday, accompanied by a note that read, "If orchids could speak, Frances, they would say we will be honored to have you wear us." They were the young woman's first.

Further, the Fourth Marine Division pitched in one hundred dollars to buy a white chiffon evening dress with a green velvet sash. Frances Newman wore it when Staff Sergeant William P. Angelos Jr. of Denver knocked on her door to serve as a proxy for her dead brother. Angelos, who had just returned from thirty-three months in the Pacific theater, took Frances dancing at the enlisted men's service club at Warner Robbins Field, Macon, Georgia. After her huge cake was cut and "Happy Birthday" sung, Frances joined her mother in a darkened corner. According to newspaper accounts, "They talked in low tones. They cried a little. Then Frances, just as General Cates had ordered, stuck out her chin and went back to the center of the party."

Frances Newman received letters and clippings from all over the United States. A week later she wrote again to General Cates—nearly five pages worth—to thank him for the flowers: "Like all fragile things, they wilted and died, but the memory of the wonderful man who gave them to me, and the darling boy who gave them to me in spirit, will linger with me always."

Frances Newman wasn't the only one who thought highly of General Clifton B. Cates. He would go on to be appointed the nineteenth commandant of the U.S. Marine Corps.

As Brother Wished

Frances & the General

again. I was just a Marine Sergeant's kid sister but I felt that I was right there when the Fighting Fourth went into battle. I was so close to Bob and I could almost feel when he went into battle. But it never occurred to me that he wouldn't come back. It was always what he was going to do when he got back.

He left a few days before my 16th birthday. He told me that on my 17th birthday he would be back. He didn't make it, but he told me when my 18th birthday came around that he would be home on furlough (he never did get one) and he would buy me a beautiful orchid, a lovely evening dress and take me dancing just as if I were his best girl. But June 13th (my 18th birthday) is not far away and I know now that he will never come back. But I'm going to buy the prettiest evening dress I can find, and I'm going dancing just as I planned. But just for a few hours, the boy I am dancing with will be Bob, come back to fill his promise. I know he'd want me to go on because we both planned on it so. The boy I go with is going to have to be awfully nice because the boy I was to have gone with was the sweetest in the world to me.

Good bye, sir, and Good Luck.

Sincerely,
Frances Newman
Duncan Hall-Room 49
Warner Robins, Georgia.

From Major General C. B. Cates to Frances Newman

HEADQUARTERS, 4TH MARINE DIVISION,
C/O FLEET POST OFFICE,
SAN FRANCISCO, CALIF.

5 MAY, 1945.

My dear Miss Newman:

May I extend to you my most heartfelt sympathy and also that of the entire Fourth Marine Division on your great loss. Your letter was received a few days ago and I have made an effort to get all the information possible pertaining to the death of your brother, Sergeant James R. Newman.

He was a scout sergeant with an assault signal unit, and landed on Iwo Jima, D Day, February 19, 1945, in the fourth wave of a reserve battalion. At the time of his death on February 23, he was in the front lines directing the fire of one of four battleships on enemy concentrations and fortifications which were hindering the advance of our men. While in a fox hole with three other men, a mortar shell exploded near it, and he was killed instantly.

In over twenty-eight years in the Marine Corps, I have received thousands of letters, but I can truthfully say yours was the most beautifully written and the finest of them all. You are a very brave young lady and the courage you are showing will be an inspiration to us all.

The lieutenant you refer to was First Lieutenant Donald N. Boydston; however, he did not go to Iwo Jima with us on account of illness, and has since been transferred to the States. Sergeant Bishop is still in the Division and he expects to write you further details soon.

My most sincere thanks for your fine letter. I have taken the liberty of showing it to members of my Staff and some civilian friends. It has touched us all deeply, very deeply, and it brought tears into my eyes as it did to each of the others. We are proud of you, Frances (if I may be so bold) and the members of the Fourth Marine Division salute you for the fortitude you are demonstrating in this hour of trial.

We will be thinking of you on your eighteenth birthday—June 13—and we wish you many happy returns. The orchids I hope to have delivered to you will be in Bob's memory. "Chin up" and a happy birthday to you, Frances Newman.

Again may I offer my condolences and hope that the knowledge that your brother died a heroic death for his country may afford you some consolation.

Sincerely,
C. B. Cates,
Major General,
U.S. Marine Corps.

A safe and a warm and a true
love ours!
There's nothing on earth to compare;
No rising crescendos
Or depths of despair
But constant, deep-rooted,
And always there!

—Loretta Sulik

Loretta Sulik wrote this poem for her sweetheart serving in the U.S. armed forces in the Pacific. It appeared in at least one newspaper and was cut out and sent to sweethearts at home and abroad.

To keep one sacred flame
Through life, unchilled unmoved,
To love in wintry age the same
As first in youth we loved,
To feel that we adore
Even to fond excess
That the heart would beat with more
It could not live without Tess.

—Thomas Moore

This poem was also printed in at least one newspaper, and clipped and sent to wartime sweethearts.

KOREA

That's All She Wrote

When I was just a lad
Before my beard turned gray,
I knew a lovely blond-haired girl,
We dated every day.

With our romance growing stronger
My love for her was high.
I knew by my draft card number
That Army days were nigh.

Instead of patiently waiting
For my greetings to come around

I joined the regular Army
As for branch I chose the ground.

She wrote to me very steadily
And she promised to be true
She said she'd wait forever
And our love would not drop through.

Then one day came a letter,
From it now I'll quote,
You should understand and pity,
For "Dear John" is all she wrote.

Published December 29, 1947, in the daily newspaper of the USAT General Patrick. The ship sailed in 19 days from Inchon, Korea to San Francisco with 1,900 troops and 100 Korean War brides on board.

Virgil & Barbara

VIRGIL PRICE enlisted in the Marine Corps in September 1946. He completed boot camp at Parris Island, South Carolina, and was assigned to that base's public information office. While serving as editor of *The Parris Island Boot*, Virgil received an early discharge to return to college and pursue a journalism degree.

At the Atlanta Division of the University of Georgia (now Georgia State University), he met high school senior Barbara Ann Showaker when she attended a college dance with a friend. Love at first sight evolved into a courtship and plans to marry. The Korean War had other plans. Virgil, now a reservist, took a college equivalency exam and was called to active duty as a second lieutenant.

Barbara's family moved to Oakland, California. He wrote many letters, like the first one here, aimed at convincing her to come back East so that they could marry before he was called to Korea. The letters were successful. Against parental objections, she flew to Washington, D.C., and the two were married at the Quantico, Virginia, post chapel on August 4, 1951.

In Korea, Virgil served as assistant historical officer for the First Marine Division. He received special orders for this duty just hours before his combat

continued on panel, next page

From Virgil Price to Barbara Ann Showaker Price

QUANTICO, VIRGINIA
JUNE 3, 1951

Barbara, sweetheart of all my dreams,
Already twice today I have written you, my darling, but I just cannot seem to get you out of my mind for a single moment. You are with me every breath I breathe, every sigh I sigh, every thought I think. Why must I be tortured so? To sit here in my lonely room and see your lovely face smile at me only to reach out for you and instead of touching the real you find instead an inanimate object—a piece of paper bearing your lovely image—the recipient of my embrace.

A man cannot live by thoughts alone even as it is said he cannot live by bread alone. You are so much a part of me that I want you by my side— in your rightful place—every minute of every hour of every day throughout eternity…

I am far from being bitter toward your parents for not granting their permission for you to come here so that we can be married now. As I have said numerous times before, I fully understand their feelings in the matter. But, as I have also said before, these are not normal times. Are we to wait an eternity for conditions to be just right for our union? Why should we be denied months of happiness together because your parents desire to view a ceremony that only lasts a few minutes?…

Please keep trying to persuade them to let you come to D.C. now. I long for you as a dying man longs for heaven. You're my everything—my very existence. Please wire me today that you are on your way and let me know if there's anything you will need. My lips burn with the fever of love that can only be cooled by your kiss.

My heart cries for you,
Virgil

KOREA – 1ST MARINE DIVISION
4 AUGUST 1952 – OUR 1ST

My darling wife,

Well, honey, this time one year ago we were in the Post Chapel at Quantico getting married. I sure wish I could be with you today so that we could celebrate together by going out to dinner, having a few cocktails and dancing. I guess we'll just have to wait until next year this time and have a double celebration.

We're having an area inspection tomorrow by the division inspector so we have spent most of the morning getting our tent and area squared away. I damn near passed out from heat exhaustion digging out my fox hole. The rains did a lot toward caving it in and also somebody had backed a truck over it, so I really had a time digging in all that rock.

Another flight element of the 23rd draft, consisting of 19 officers, got in this morning, and they threw noon chow out of whack again so that when I got there they'd run out of meat loaf and were serving Spam <u>again.</u>

Yesterday I got to thinking about all the plans I'd made for when I get back to the states and get out, and I thought of how selfish I'd been, giving you hardly any voice in the matter at all. I know you've said that if I wanted to go back to school you'd work until I finished, and you've also stated your desire to have a few little Barbara's and Virgil's as soon as possible, but that's about the extent of it. Now I'd really like to know what your honest wishes in the matter are. Do you think you'd be as happy if we settled in Atlanta, or had you rather we settle somewhere nearer your folks? Seriously, I'd like to have you voice your opinions on this and please feel free to say anything you think. You know I'd be happy any-

outfit was to head back to the front line. He had been serving as platoon commander of the First Platoon, How Company, Third Battalion, First Marine Regiment.

Virgil and Barbara returned to Georgia, where the war veteran finally did receive that degree in journalism from the University of Georgia, Athens. They later moved to Tampa, Florida, where Virgil worked as director of advertising and public relations for the Tampa Electric Company. This photo of the Price family was taken in Tampa in 1957.

The couple enjoyed twenty-six years of marriage, including two sons and two daughters, before Barbara suffered cardiac arrest and died in November 1977, a month shy of her forty-fifth birthday. Virgil remained in the Marine Corps Reserve, retiring at his own request in May 1973 as lieutenant colonel. He lives in Inverness, Florida.

Virgil & Barbara

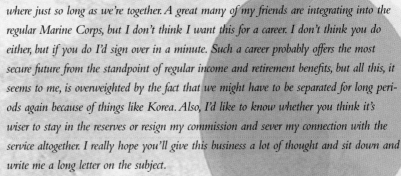

where just so long as we're together. A great many of my friends are integrating into the regular Marine Corps, but I don't think I want this for a career. I don't think you do either, but if you do I'd sign over in a minute. Such a career probably offers the most secure future from the standpoint of regular income and retirement benefits, but all this, it seems to me, is overweighted by the fact that we might have to be separated for long periods again because of things like Korea. Also, I'd like to know whether you think it's wiser to stay in the reserves or resign my commission and sever my connection with the service altogether. I really hope you'll give this business a lot of thought and sit down and write me a long letter on the subject.

I hope you that you will always feel like a bride sweetheart, no matter how old we both get or how many kids we do decide to have. We'll just have to make sure that we don't get in a rut. We'll go out dining and dancing as often as possible. We'll fix us up a place to play games and go swimming and play tennis a lot to keep in good health always.

I promise to always be a kind, thoughtful and considerate husband, keeping in mind always the "little things" that you keep reminding me are so important. I hope to never forget your birthday, our anniversary or any of the other dates that are important in our lives. I promise to work hard and to do everything to give you a nice home for you to keep for us and bring up our kids in, and I think we will both find life so much happier no matter where we are just so we're together.

There are so many other things I'd like to say tonight, my darling, but I just can't seem to get them down on paper, so I'll close for now with a very Happy Anniversary to you, Mrs. Price.

Your loving husband,
Virgil

VIETNAM

Taisau

I went to a bar 'way down by the track
There stood a co dep, long hair down her back
Her eyes, how they sparkled in response to my touch
I told her I loved her, I loved her too much

Hey you! Come in. Sit down. What's your name?
How long have you been in Viet Nam?
I've been in your country the whole live-long day
So sit right down by me and hear what I say

I'm tired of drinking your old bamuyba
I'm tired of fighting your old war
I'm packing my bags and I'm going back home
To my sweet little Vickie, the girl I adore.

BARRACKS SONG OF AMERICAN GI'S IN VIETNAM

Jon & Kay

From Jon Christian Merkel to Kay Merkel

4 July 68

Hi Love,

Happy 4th of July. No fireworks in these parts although some have been expected. Nothing but the usual B-52s dropping bombs, 20 or 30 miles from here, on the VC positions. Sounds like the rolling distant thunder of a summer rainstorm…

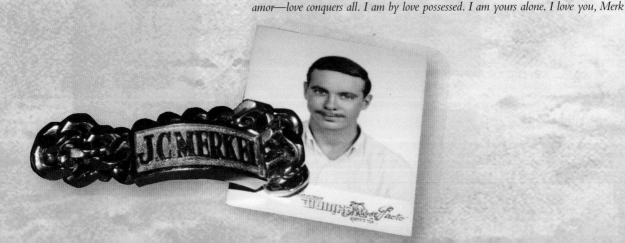

17 JULY 68

…Thought for the day: Love pushes aside the bitter findings of experience. Love knows for a fact that which is not a fact; with ease, love believes the unbelievable; love wishes and makes it so. Moreover, where love's weakness seems to be, love's strength resides. Itself all unreality, love is assailed by reality in vain. You might as well wound the loud winds, kill the still closing waters. Omnia vincit amor—love conquers all. I am by love possessed. I am yours alone. I love you, Merk

JON AND KAY MERKEL married in 1967. The following year, Kay went to live in Bangkok while Jon went to Saigon to investigate the living conditions following the Tet offensive. Jon's letters encouraged his young wife to be brave living in a huge metropolis, and to join him in the war zone. Once both in Saigon, life was surprisingly normal. Kay taught school while Jon flew helicopters.

In the fall of 1969, they were transferred to Udorn, Thailand, where Jon flew into Laos. Three months later he was killed. Air America told Kay not to discuss his death with anyone for security reasons, but she found it headlined in the *New York Times* at the Frankfurt airport.

Kay Merkel Boruff lives in Dallas and has taught at the prestigious Hockaday School for twenty-four years.

Chuck & Carol

From Charles Shahan to Carol Shoemaker Shahan

6 JAN. 67

Dear Carol,

Well Honey, here's my first letter to you and I don't know of any better way to start it except with, I LOVE YOU.

Our mail will stay aboard the ship till we get to Hawaii, so you won't get this for awhile. I won't get any mail till then either. Just remember I'm writing even if you don't get my letters regularly.

It was really rough leaving you yesterday. I just didn't want to let you go or say good-bye. I'll admit I had butterflies in my stomach and I felt like letting the tears come. I guess it's because I love you so much. Now I'm thinking about us getting married when I get home. It's a long time away, but I know it'll go by fast for me.

In four days we'll be in Hawaii. I'm only gonna leave the boat long enough to call you. I hope I can get a hold of you. After Hawaii we go to Yokosuka, Japan and I'll buy our silverware.

We're having promotions in the morning and I hope I'll have good news for you when I write tomorrow night. I sure hope I make Corporal, cause the extra money will sure come in handy. We're gonna need quite a lot when we get married, but I know we can make it o.k. First thing I want to do is get your ring paid for, which shouldn't take me too long.

After I finish this letter I'll write the folks and tell them we're getting married as soon as I get back. I doubt if it'll come as much of a surprise to them.

I've already started on my plan to gain weight. I've been eating like crazy and I quit drinking coffee. That may be hard to believe, but it's true! I don't even want any coffee. I know I'll feel better now that I quit and that I'm eating more. I'll keep you informed on how I'm doing.

I doubt if I'll ever catch up on my letter writing. I've got to thank people for Xmas cards they sent me and I've got to answer Dick + Jackie's letter too. Don't worry, your letter will always be the first one I write. I love you + miss you very deeply Carol. All I'm looking forward to is coming home to you. I never thought I could love someone so much as I do you. I'll sure be glad when this is all over and we can get married and spend the rest of our lives together.

I guess I'd better go for now. I've gotta write and tell the folks about us getting married when I get back. I hope you tell your folks soon.

Tell your folks and all your relatives hi for me and tell your Grandmother a special hello. Just remember I love you and miss you with all my heart.

Love Always,

Chuck

P.S. More Than Yesterday,

Less Than Tomorrow.

Because my love for you is always growing.

Missouri native Charles "Chuck" Shahan served in the U.S. Marine Corps from 1964 to 1968, leaving as a sergeant. From 1965 to 1967, he served sea duty aboard the U.S.S. *Hancock*. He disliked being shipboard, saying he "was a marine and should be fighting on land."

Chuck asked Californian Carol Shoemaker to marry him before leaving for a second tour. Through letters, he postponed the wedding because he was worried about being sent back to Vietnam and leaving a new wife behind. Carol thought he got cold feet. They would laugh about it years later.

The couple married July 22, 1967, the day Chuck arrived home. They had two sons, one who followed in his father's footsteps as a marine. Twenty days short of their twenty-fifth wedding anniversary, Chuck Shahan passed away.

Chuck & Carol

7 MAY 67

Dear Carol,

I got your letter dated May 2nd today. I know you're upset and postponing the wedding will upset you a lot more, but we've got to wait till I get out of the Marines. I wish to God that we'd waited till later to make all these plans.

It'd be so much better for us, cause being married and being in the service just won't work. I wish I'd listened to your Dad. It'd take all the money I make and you'd have to work too, just to live. If we wait I'll have a little more money in the bank and we could start out like a newly married couple should. Please try to understand.

The reason I want my rings back is because I want you to date around and not be tied down while I'm at Pendleton or wherever I'm at. This way if you find someone else you won't be obligated to me.

Carol we've got to be reasonable about this. I'm not gonna be married and only see my wife 3 or 4 days a week or leave her to go back overseas. When we get married it'll be when I'm thru with my military obligation and I can come home every night. I'll also have a job and enough money to live comfortably.

Carol I know you'll be hurt, but you've got to understand that it'll be so much better if we wait. Believe me, this sure as hell isn't easy for me, but we have to postpone it.

Like a friend of our family once said to me, "if she loves you now, she'll love you that much more when you get out." I hope this is true.

Please Carol, don't hate me or anything like that, just try and understand it's best for both of us. If we're really meant for each other things will work out. If your love is as strong for me as you think, you should be willing to wait.

I can't explain it any better, I just hope you understand.

Love always,
Chuck

Jim & his parents

From James L. Young to his parents

APRIL 3, 1969

Dear Folks,

It's thirty minutes into a new day now. The moon is full tonight and shadows are passing swiftly over the camp as the clouds move overhead. Outside the door, five choppers are sitting silently looking somewhat like giant grasshoppers silhouetted against the glow of the lights surrounding the camp. The squared sandbag bunkers stand out like towers on a medieval castle. Simon and Garfunkel are singing earnestly though the speakers of a tape recorder, accompanied by the sounds of mortars and artillery exploding on some distant hill. Somewhere, many many miles from here a good friend is sleeping on the damp jungle floor or maybe he is running now, desperately hoping that the next bullet will not catch him.

In a few days or possibly weeks, we will change places, but one tries not to think of such things. Last week two friends did not come back laughing. You wonder if your friends out there tonight will come back laughing. You hope—Such as it is as the minutes move into the first hour of a new day.—Kontum, Vietnam

JIM YOUNG arrived in South Vietnam December 5, 1968, a single, twenty-four-year-old second lieutenant. By virtue of his special forces (Green Beret) training, he was assigned to Command and Control Central, Military Assistance Command Vietnam (CCC, MAC-V SOG). He was leader of Recon Team Arizona; his code name was King Arthur.

Jim's older brother Bob was a Presbyterian minister serving in Gastonia, North Carolina. Thinking that his little brother needed inspiration, he circulated the lieutenant's address and social security number among the young ladies of his church. Candy Shermer, a student at Medical College of Virginia in Richmond, Virginia, would become King Arthur's lady.

Jim&Candy

From James L. Young
to Candy Shermer Young

OCT. 23, 1969

…Candy, your letter was a pleasant surprise—especially the means that you received my address—I am rather surprised at Bob handing our family secrets out on index cards— but you might be interested to know that I am happy that he did…

After exchanging a few letters, they met in person during Jim's Christmas leave. He was awed by her beautiful red hair—and short miniskirt: "I was thunderstruck." He had already volunteered for a second tour in Vietnam. He would serve three.

APRIL 2ND, 1970
11:30 P.M.

Dearest Candy,

First, I must confess that I am not in the best of spirits to be writing this letter. The reasons are many and varied and I hesitate to even attempt to explain. I don't know if you have been caught up in the wave of emotions that seem to be rising in the States concerning the numerous situations that are arising elsewhere in the world—and perhaps it is possibly best that I do not know and it is possible that I may not even care. Candy do not feel that my bitterness is directed toward you…

A week, maybe two weeks ago—it's hard to really remember any one day—I received your letter in answer more or less to my last. My first impulse was to throw it away—Now before your hate reaches a climax, let me relate what had happened just prior to my opening your letter.

Jim&Candy

HISTORICAL NOTE

Special forces is the elite branch of the army, called Green Berets because of their distinctive uniform.

Many people die here, but some more than others. I had had maybe four, five hours sleep in two days—what I was doing is not too important—but a close friend of mine and others with him were in a situation that I had been in before—I was above him in a plane for the better part of two days—I listened to the panic in his voice over the radio and I felt the same fear he felt—but Jerry never knew this. I had to talk to him in a matter of fact voice—the mission needed to be done—keep him going—we kept him going for two days—pushing him to his limits—When he finally reached the stage where you could not push anymore—he had done all that could be done—Oh the hell with all this, the chopper he was coming home on was blown up - bang - exploded - all dead - just a few hours before I read your letter.

I am sorry Candy, these last few pages do not read too well. It has been very busy and tiring since I returned a few months ago. I did not think it could get worse, but these last few weeks have proven me wrong. There have been many more times like the last—two nights ago there were sappers in the camp—and a few more of us are not here—today, two more have gone and I am really getting sick with myself tonight. What would you have me to do Candy? Never write this way? Never have I before—but then if I did not, you would never know that I did—so I think I will let this be as it is. Christ…

I feel something very, very strong now and it seems so urgent. You said that you were afraid of this, if it be one in the same, being shallow and cannot last. I have tried to relax for the last few moments—but to no success—to me it is not important that it be there tomorrow—but to what is here now—now while I am writing this letters—what I say today, I mean today—today is today—too many things change for tomorrow to always be like today. If of course you never hear from me again, you will know that it was today that you were important.——And Candy the problems you are having are not being forgotten by me—you are my dear a totally exceptional wonder—and I wonder not that you will walk over your mountains—To lecture and say what one should do is not the way that I do—but a smile is yours and a lot of love today is yours and a lot of things that do not have names are yours and today they are from me—to end is not sufficient, but I will subside—

Jim

MAY 14, 1970
10:15 P.M.

…There's a beach with a warm white sand; a cool ocean breeze; a soft quiet sunset; There is the cold wet splash of the water against our legs as we walk in the surf's edge—Sometimes there is a puppy dancing at our feet; Sometimes there are seagulls floating on the breeze; Always our hands are locked together; Always she is laughing. And Candy you are always that lovely girl…

DECEMBER 6, 1970
2:30 SUNDAY

…I don't know if you can see it in my eyes, but each one of these pictures shows me thinking of you saying, saying to myself, "Damn Young, you love that girl, don't you …"

DECEMBER 25, 1970
1 A.M.

Darling,
I have been dreaming that … Somewhere it is Christmas … Christmas as it should be. We are together … your head is resting on my chest; my arm is around your shoulders; and your hair is tickling my nose.

> *The house isn't really very large or different and some may even call it a cottage.*
> *Outside it is cold… it snowed last night. The pines and firs are white on this morning. There are small black shadows in the snow left earlier by a rabbit; probably a snow rabbit.*
> *And as we look through the window at the snow as it slopes down the hill and meets the lake; you tell the window how pretty the snow is today. I squeeze your shoulder and with my lips to your ear I whisper…I love you.*
> *You turn and look at me wondering why I am looking at you and not the snow. I kiss your lips once, twice … I love you.*

> *This may all very well be a childlike fantasy; but it is a fantasy that I want to last forever; a fantasy that seems so very real … even now.*
> *Candy, if I could and if they were mine, I would give away the heavens to be with you now. I miss you very deeply—No one is loved as I love you.*

Jim

JIM YOUNG married Candy Shermer on New Year's Eve 1971. They stood in two feet of snow outside an old stone church in West Boylston, Massachusetts, in the presence of the Special Forces Tenth Group SCUBA Team. He left the army the following year.

Jim Young was honored with a Purple Heart, the Bronze Star, and the Vietnamese Cross of Gallantry for his three tours of service. He left the awards at the Virginia War Memorial in protest of then president-elect Jimmy Carter's proposed blanket pardon to draft resisters and military deserters.

Today Jim is an insurance examiner and Candy teaches fifth grade. They have two daughters and live in Midlothian, Virginia. Jim's Vietnam experience has helped focus his family's values on duty and honor. Over the years they have had many discussions on the veterans missing in action and the draft-dodging of the time. Jim and Candy have written several letters to the editor concerning Vietnam issues. One of Jim's was named among *USA Today's* top five letters to the editor of 1992.

Thirteen Christmases ago, Jim discovered he had a natural talent as an artist and today "K. Arthur" carries his Vietnam legacy to future generations through wood carvings.

THE PERSIAN GULF

Day after day I stand in line.
But every so often there's nothing I find.
My friends feel the warmth, of word faraway,
But I feel no warmth; no words for me to say.

The loneliness I feel, with the void that I'm in
Makes me wonder why, this had to begin
To be in a country, in another strange land
As I dream of this lady, when we walked hand in hand.

As I sit here and think of the time left to kill
Just remember I love you, and I always will.

LLOYD A. AUCOIN III

Lloyd&Kim

From Lloyd A. Aucoin III to Kimberley Leach Aucoin

17 SEPT. [1990]

Dear Kim,

Well another day has come and gone, without any mail. I wish I knew what was going on. I'm sure there's a good explanation, but every time I don't get any letter my insides start eating me up. The other night I went to church (Protestant, because I missed Catholic services) I prayed that everything was all right…I still have that little bracelet tied to my ankle, and in my hand I'm holding the seashell and your class ring you gave me. I hold them in my hands when I'm thinking of you to give me comfort I guess. They're about the only things I have here besides your picture to keep me company…

24 SEPT. [1990]

My Dearest Kim,

Well my love it seems pretty hard to believe that I've been here a month already. It seems like I've been here forever...The only thing I wish is that the time would pass by faster. I overheard a rumor about an attack that was supposed to take place within the next couple of weeks but that's all I'm going to say. It may just be a rumor but when or if it happens maybe you won't be so surprised. I hope something would happen soon because that'll be the only way we get out of here faster. I think this standoff has gone on long enough. You know it seems strange about how I was never scheduled to come out here and I end up being on the first plane to arrive in country. But one thing you should know baby. No matter what goes on around here I still think of you quite often. Some nights I dream about what our wedding will be like and other nights I dream of everything we did when you came home on leave. Just think my love in about a month and a half we'll have known each other for a whole year. The one thing do know my love is that our relationship has traveled over some rough roads being apart from each other, and it may look like we'll have to travel over a few more before this is all over. I miss you terribly baby, even more so now than ever. I can hardly wait until the day when you'll be mine forever...

LLOYD A. AUCOIN III and Kimberley Leach, both marines, met at Marine Corps Air Station El Toro, California, in November 1989. Kimberley was transferred to Okinawa soon after. During a leave-time reunion at El Toro, the two became engaged; but Uncle Sam would make planning a wedding quite a challenge.

Lloyd was called to Operation Desert Shield less than two weeks after Kimberley returned to Okinawa. (Kimberley's former Marine Corps band unit would also be going to the Persian Gulf.) Although marines had the capability to call home while in Saudi Arabia, the calls had to be collect. Kimberley couldn't receive any collect calls in Japan, so mail was their only means of communication—slow mail. Kimberley's letters took up to four weeks to reach her fiancé, who worried, and wondered, and waited.

Lloyd served as motor transport mechanic in Saudi Arabia from August 1990 until May 1991. Six weeks before Kimberley was due to transfer back to California, this time to the First Marine Division Band at Camp Pendleton, she was involuntarily extended for an additional six months. It would be July 31, 1991, before the couple reunited.

They wasted no time in marrying November 1991. Lloyd now serves as maintenance chief at The Basic School and as a drill instructor at Officer Candidate School. Kimberley is assistant to the director of marine corps music. They live in Northern Virginia with their sons, L. Adrien Aucoin I, and Alexander Wallace Aucoin.

Roy & Kathy

Between Roy Bolar
and Kathy Higdon Bolar

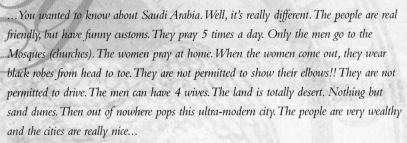

OCT. 19, 1990

…You wanted to know about Saudi Arabia. Well, it's really different. The people are real friendly, but have funny customs. They pray 5 times a day. Only the men go to the Mosques (churches). The women pray at home. When the women come out, they wear black robes from head to toe. They are not permitted to show their elbows!! They are not permitted to drive. The men can have 4 wives. The land is totally desert. Nothing but sand dunes. Then out of nowhere pops this ultra-modern city. The people are very wealthy and the cities are really nice…

…I hope you don't mind, but I showed your picture to some guys in our tent. Needless to say, we were all blown away!! We've been here for 60 days and haven't seen a woman's elbow, so you were really a breath of fresh air. You are a really good-looking young lady!! Well, I gotta go. But first I want to thank you for taking the time to write. I know it must really be hectic in your first year of college. But it really means a lot to get mail, for a soldier. Especially from someone who seems as nice as you. You take care of yourself. Study hard and BE ALL YOU CAN BE. Seems like I've heard that somewhere before. Ha ha. Write back whenever you can. Your Pal, Roy

16 NOV. 90

…Well, we got some bad news today. We just got our orders to move. We're heading up farther north. We'll be pretty close to the Iraq border. But that's where they need us most I guess there have been some strong rumors of an American offensive starting after the holidays. It sounds logical. I don't think the American people back in the states would like to receive a bunch of body bags for Christmas. This is just a reality that we face. If there is a war, many soldiers will be killed. We know that, but the American public doesn't want to

see that. Well enough about this subject. I hope I don't depress you when I talk about this subject. But sometimes it's good for us to talk about it to someone. I hope you don't mind…

24 NOV. 90

…So how did you spend your Thanksgiving? Did you have a good time? I hope you did. How is school coming? Have you found your Prince Charming yet? As nice and as beautiful as you are, the Prince will be getting a Queen…

5 DEC. 90

…We had an exciting morning Sunday. We woke up to a chemical attack alarm. They told us Iraq had fired missiles in our direction and they would hit in 20 minutes. So we all got into our "chemical protective outer garments," put on our mask and waited. Well, thank God they never did. What happened was, the Iraqis were having a military exercise and our radars picked up the missiles being fired. But Iraq shot the missiles down before they crossed into Saudi Arabian air space…Nothing like a nice missile raid in the morning! Ha ha. But everything is fine…

You asked in one of your letters if I am throwing your letters out or am I keeping them. I have kept every one of them. Sometimes when I don't get mail, I get them out and read them again. I don't know why. I know them all by heart anyways. But I keep all the letters that everyone has written. They will be interesting to read after all this is over and I'm back in the states again…

Kathy Higdon's first letter to "Any Serviceman" ended up in the hands of a married serviceman. He thought she sounded nice and forwarded it to a single high school buddy, Roy Bolar.

Roy was a Fort Bragg, North Carolina–based operating room technician with the Fifth Mobile Army Surgical Hospital. Kathy was a freshman at Northwest Missouri State University. She and her Delta Zeta sorority sisters wrote several members of Roy's company. But no other pen pals hit it off like they did.

Roy came calling eight days after returning from the Persian Gulf. After an awkward first meeting, in the same dorm room in which Kathy got word that the United States had bombed Iraq, the couple hit it off. The next month, Roy and Kathy went to a local lake to feed the ducks. Hidden in the bag of bread was an engagement ring. Two years later, on June 5, 1993, they wed.

Kathy gave birth to Jacob Bolar on May 19, 1996. Roy, after earning a degree in government, reentered the army the same year as a second lieutenant.

Roy&Kathy

From Kathy

1-16-91

...It is 6:14pm. News is on + we just bombed Iraq. I'm scared...When you come home, I might - well, probably, will want you just to hold me for an hour or two. Is that crazy to ask? Am I too forward? I don't care...I don't really care if I am too forward, because I am afraid. Promise me you won't laugh when I just need to be held - please. Roy, promise me also that you'll be careful + you'll come see me. I'm waiting...remember how you said it's not right to ask someone to wait? Well, you didn't ask...remember that.

JAN. 18, 1991 8:53 PM

Hi Doll!
How are you? Safe and happy I hope! I'm fine - trying to learn as much about the war + trying not to worry!

It seems all I've done is sit and veg out in front of the TV waiting for news. My schoolwork seems so unimportant. It's weird, but I'm thinking to my future. I mean, if I have children one day + they come home from school + say, "Mom, do you remember 'Operation Desert Storm'?" I want to be able to say, "Yes, + this is what happened..." Does that make sense? My Mom can't tell me much about Vietnam—I don't want to be like that. I'm saving newspapers and all, maybe that will help my children understand. Wish I understood more about Vietnam!

I'm wearing a yellow ribbon tied around my ankle. (I wear too many bracelets + it got all tangled up!) and I have a yellow ribbon I pin on the outside of all my clothing. When you come home, you can remove the one around my ankle—I'll wear it until you come home...it will not be removed until them. Same goes for the ribbon on my clothing.

I'm trying to locate your parents just to be in touch. I found Aberdeen + there are two "Bolars," but both are unlisted—is that not my luck or what? I'll keep you filled in...

Tomorrow, I'm going to AT&T + try + get something faxed to you! You'll have to let me know if it works!

HISTORICAL NOTE

Roy Bolar's MASH unit moved from Dhahran into Iraq during the ground offensive. It lasted only four days. Iraq's ground forces had already been beaten badly by U.S. bombing missions, and surviving troops began surrendering by the tens of thousands. By February 27, President George Bush announced that he had ordered a cease-fire.

John & Joy

From Staff Sergeant John Chavez to Joy Erdy Chavez

18 OCT. 90 0800

Hi Joy

My name is John Chavez. I'm 28 years old, I left Myrtle Beach about 55 days ago and so far it hasn't gotten any better...I'm tired of waiting for something to happen. I'm about one hundred and twenty miles away from Kuwait, three minutes by missile, five minutes by plane and eight hours by tank, but my two friends will always be by my side when that hour approaches, my M-16 and my trusted gas mask. Joy so you're twenty-seven, I love blue eyes, would I be asking too much if I said I wanted a picture of you? Maybe I can look you up when I get back if my Porsche is still running...

After seeing a newspaper story about the Persian Gulf conflict in September 1990, Joy Erdy wrote a letter to "Any Service Member." Not just any service member answered. Staff Sergeant John Chavez, U.S. Air Force, picked Joy's letter from a boxful because he liked her handwriting. He just happened to be based in Myrtle Beach, hours from her Fort Mill, South Carolina, home. She was twenty-seven, he was twenty-eight.

They wrote about their families, and their fears, and the chance that being pen pals could evolve into something else after the war. He didn't have a picture of himself to send—so he mailed her his driver's license. John Chavez served from August 1990 to March 20, 1991, his birthday. Two weeks later, after their first face-to-face meeting, he wrote a marriage proposal to Joy in the sand of Myrtle Beach. They have a thirteen-year-old adopted son, Jonathan, and reside in Rock Hill, South Carolina.

18 Nov. 90 0640

…The days have cooled off considerably and the nights are even colder. I wish I could cuddle up with you, but your letters will have to do for now. They keep me going…Joy I have all the pictures you sent me. I like the one where you're in the black dress with blue sleeves. I love your Dimples…

5 Dec. 90 9:00 PM

You made my day. I can't believe I'm hearing your voice. I love your Southern accent. I don't know what to say to keep you…Your TAPE, I still can't get over it, that country bumpkin accent, I love it. I put my headphones on and it's as if I was with you. I keep playing it over and over. I just close my eyes and lay on my cot listening to your voice. I can't wait to get out of here to meet you…

9 Dec. 90 11:00 PM

…You know last week Iraq shot a missile that traveled 350 miles in 7 minutes and everyone over here took 10 minutes to react to it. We would have been deader than door-knobs to say the least. We all carry our gas masks everywhere. It's real scary when our leaders take this long to pass the word down to the Indians (us). I just hope I'm fast enough to put my gear on when the time comes…

4 JAN 91

…I received your package on the 12th. I ran to my place of work to enjoy a few private minutes before everyone could get there. I was beginning to believe that you had forgotten me. I was/am ecstatic. I feel like yelling out loud just because…I'm very fortunate to have met you by correspondence. I can't wait to meet you in person, hopefully not later than March, that's what we were told, God willing, of course. Thank you for my present and the shirt with our names, and your picture, which I keep next to my bible…

Love,

Joy

MAP OF MY HEART

X

…AND HERE!

Happy Holidays

U.S. Central Air Forces
Operation Desert Shield

December 25, 1990

John & Joy

19 JAN 91

Hi baby

Don't worry. I'm doing as best I can. Well, what can I say, war broke out Thursday at 1:00 o'clock in the morning, but we were in our chemical gear at 11:00 o'clock Wednesday night. All the lights went out and everything went silent, then all of a sudden F-16s started taking off, one after another. They looked like shooting stars because all you could see were their engines flame out. I felt excited, scared and relieved at the same time, one day closer to going home. Friday the 18th the alarm sounded at 6:00 a.m. I was caught without my gear on. Hell that night before I took a shower and decided to rest a few minutes before getting into that bulky gear. Well to say the least I never woke up till the alarm sounded. You know I moved pretty fast that time, I was amazed. Now when I go to bed I sleep with my gear and boots on, so all I have to do is grab my gas mask and run into the bunker. As extra precaution we were vaccinated against anthrax plus we are also taking nerve agent tablets every 8 hours. Side effects are vomiting, blurred vision and diarrhea, but who knows what else might develop years from now. We also carry atropine injections in our gas mask bag. In case we do get slimed and I start twitching, 6 of these puppies should do the job.

Everything is quiet around here, no terrorist attacks yet, I hope it stays like this until that madman gives up or we drop one on his head...

5 FEB. 91

...Today Iraq shot an A-10 aircraft down. The airplane belonged to England AFB Louisiana. Just like that, you see the pilots eating in the chow hall then the next day

they just cease to exist. It's unbelievable. I guess the pilots do have the right to brag and be cocky. also a few days ago an AC-30 aircraft was also shot down; 14 aircrew members were in it. You know life goes on as if nothing ever happened. May God help their families through their ordeal…

16 MAR 91

We are finally getting closer to going home. All of the bunkers have been taken down and every piece of wooden furniture had to be taken out from all the tents, so whenever you get the word all you have to do is fold your cot and tear down your tent. Yesterday the hospital left for Myrtle beach. I was very jealous but what the hell, my turn will come. Our commander said that everyone from Myrtle Beach should be home before the end of this month. Yeah, Fantastic, I CAN'T WAIT. I hope everything works out between us. I still can't believe I spoke to you. WOW! … afterwards, I didn't know whether to cry, laugh or do back flips.

HISTORICAL NOTE

The Persian Gulf War brought John and Joy Chavez together. It also brought them plenty of pain—physical pain. John began getting sick in Kuwait, and when he came home, fevers, headaches, sinus problems, rashes, and fatigue followed. The next year brought brittle teeth, joint pain, and short-term memory loss. When they first met, Joy had constantly watering eyes. After they married, she too experienced brittle teeth, headaches, and John's other ailments.

In early 1993, the Chavezes founded Gulf War Veterans of the Carolinas, a support group for those suffering with similar symptoms, known collectively as Gulf War syndrome. Across the country, thousands of Gulf War veterans and their spouses and their children are exhibiting similar signs. They believe the illness is the result of exposure to chemical agents used during the war. So far, however, doctors have yet to find a single cause of the mystery ailment to support the existence of Gulf War syndrome.

According to the department of Veterans Affairs, more than 153,000 Gulf War disability cases were pending as of April 1996. (That number is about one-third of the total who served in the war.)